I have desperately searched for the "gospel" about in *Hope and Holiness*. John brings his breadth of theology about the power of the Holy Spirit to the timely topic of sexual holiness. Using 1 Corinthians 6 as his starting point, he unpacks a way for sexual purity that challenges the old "do more" and "try harder" approaches. This book contains the most liberating message the world has ever heard—that God wants "us" before He wants our behavior, and when He has us, our changed hearts respond with love and obedience. I don't know of another book that addresses sexual purity with such clarity and Christ-centered convictions. I believe God will use this book to bring hope and healing to performance-weary Christians who need to know and grow in the constancy of God's love.

CHUCK COLLINS, director, Center for Reformation Anglicanism

What does it take to have real victory over sexual sin? Here John Fonville calls out the church's flailing attempts to help those ravaged by pornography and other destructive habits—and lights a path toward true transformation through the power of God.

ERIC METAXAS, #1 *New York Times* bestselling author and host of the nationally syndicated *Eric Metaxas Radio Show*

This important book tackles what is perhaps the greatest enemy facing Christians today. Sexual sin is nothing new, but the epidemic of pornography and its consequences have devastated the church and ruined the lives and ministries of pastors from every denomination. John Fonville knows that there is no miracle cure for this disease, but he develops a strategy for combating it that is firmly grounded in biblical principles and practical application. It is a manual of self-discipline rooted in submission to the Word of God and a close relationship with Jesus Christ, and very much needed by everyone active in church life today.

GERALD BRAY, research professor of divinity, Beeson Divinity School

We live in a culture that calls good evil and evil good (Isa. 5:18–24). Truth has stumbled in the streets and those who hold to it make themselves a prey (Isa. 59:12–14). Could it be why America is self-destructing and inviting the just judgment of God? John's shepherding heart and biblical approach to the rampant problem of immorality and the distortion of biblical morality lays the foundation that will help the reader practically and personally experience the power of the gospel over sin. Don't just read what John writes in *Hope and Holiness*—study it with an open Bible. Mark the text. Watch how God sends His Word to heal us and deliver us from all our destructions (Ps. 107:20).

KAY ARTHUR, cofounder, Brand Ambassador, Precept; author, *The Truth about Sex*

There is no more thorny issue for the contemporary Christian disciple than that of sexual sin and temptation. With pastoral insight and theological acuity, John Fonville shows us that it is the gospel itself that is the sweetest remedy for our hurts—the power of God to save us and to sanctify us. The tender counsel of this book will be a mercy both to Christians and those who seek to shepherd them.

MICHAEL P. JENSEN, rector, St Mark's Anglican Church, Darling Point, Sydney

The topic of sexual purity is increasingly relevant. Many books attempt to defend a biblical sexual ethnic by emphasizing God's law and man's need to obey. Others abandon culturally "outdated" beliefs such as monogamy and "saving yourself" for marriage in favor of acceptance and cheap grace. Christians are often caught between rules without grace and grace without rules. John Fonville brings us back to the gospel in response to both extremes. The gospel calls us to God-honoring behavior and empowers us to obey. Because we have been set free from the power of sin, we are free to struggle against our sin. Knowing we are forgiven, we can cast off shame and learn to live in light of who we are in Christ. I look forward to seeing how God blesses His church through this book.

RACHEL MILLER, author of *Beyond Authority and Submission: Women and Men in Marriage, Church, and Society*

Why do Christians struggle with sexual immorality? What is the Christian's pathway to living a life of purity? Does God expect of us something that is impossible? Author John Fonville answers these questions and others in *Hope and Holiness*. I highly recommend this book to anyone who seeks to honor God by living a life of purity.

GARY CHAPMAN, author of *The 5 Love Languages*

John Fonville boldly speaks of sexual immorality, indicating a divine standard for human sexual conduct, but at the same time he calls for grace in dealing with sexual immorality within the church and a grace-informed disposition toward sexually immoral unbelievers that calls us to see them as equal image-bearers of God who are our neighbors and whom we are required to love. Fonville is faithful in upholding the sanctity of both law and gospel in a most critical aspect of the human experience. I highly recommend this work.

KENNETH R. JONES, pastor, Glendale Baptist Church, Miami, FL

John Fonville's book, *Hope and Holiness*, is a seminal and important book. The church in the West is being weakened and undermined, seemingly unable to resist the onslaught of sexual permissiveness. Many remedies have been tried and, more often than not, failed. Fonville argues that many of the so-called therapies "tear down" rather than "build up" as they promote confidence in the self rather than in Christ. What is needed is a deeper grasp of the gospel, which alone has the power to engender holiness. Essentially an exposition of 1 Corinthians 6, Fonville's book points us to the way in which a deeper grasp of the gospel is our only hope in a culture that has given itself over to unanchored sexual desire. I read this book with increasing excitement and hope and came away refreshed. I recommend it unreservedly.

NIGEL ATKINSON, vicar, St John's Knutsford and Toft, Diocese of Chester, England

When the world is more and more aggressively seeking to pressure Christians to conform their teaching, morals, and behavior to its godless standards, the importance of carefully argued cases for the maintenance of biblical values has never been greater. When so many church leaders and teachers are proclaiming the necessity for Christians to follow the world's lead in the downward rush to sexual and moral impurity, we need to revisit Paul's injunction that we should not be conformed to the world but be transformed by the renewal of our minds (Rom. 12:2). When the faculty members of far too many theological colleges seem to be dedicated to teaching their students godless reasons why they should not believe the Bible, we need to spare no effort to proclaim the glories of the Christ, who is the central content of the Bible. John Fonville's study, focusing mainly on the teaching of Paul in his first epistle to the Corinthians, is a timely response to secular society's growing rejection of God's revealed will regarding sexual behavior, gender identity, and marriage. This is a timely reminder of the clear biblical teaching about the implications of the gospel for the way we regard and use our bodies.

GRAEME GOLDSWORTHY, former lecturer in Old Testament, Biblical Theology, and Hermeneutics at Moore Theological College, Sydney

I congratulate my friend John Fonville on this outstanding and much-needed book. The reader is taken on a journey to appreciate how the apostle Paul's gospel ministry to the Corinthian church in the first-century AD is just as relevant for us today as it was for them then. This book will empower many in sexual purity by redirecting the disempowered away from a toothless principle-driven approach to the engine room of Christ, the gospel, and resulting life by the Spirit. I highly recommend this work.

JASON SHIELS, pastor of Liberty Church, Mid-Ulster (Northern Ireland)

With conviction and clarity, John Fonville walks his readers through Paul's repeated question to the Corinthians, "Do you not know?" and shows how only the gospel—God's gracious act of salvation through His Son Jesus Christ—can free us from sexual immorality.

ZAC NEUBAUER, president of the US chapter of the Evangelical Fellowship in the Anglican Communion

In the sensitive subject of Christian sexuality, John Fonville leads us back to the fountains of faith. With the book of 1 Corinthians and basic principles of the Reformation, John Fonville shows hope for the sexually hopeless.

FABIAN MEDERACKE, pastor at the St. Mary's Lutheran City church of Wittenberg, the mother church of the Reformation

How can Christians find, keep, and enjoy sexual purity in a sex-crazed culture (first-century Corinth or twenty-first-century America)? Steps, programs, regret, fear of discovery, and will-power may apply *brakes* that slow the heart's momentum toward shameful fantasies and deeds. But they cannot *break* the tyranny of lust. Paul showed the Christians of Corinth that *only the grace of God in Christ*—redeeming, forgiving, transforming grace—can actually break the power of reigning sin and set its captives free. John Fonville's *Hope and Holiness* opens up for us, clearly, deeply, and movingly, the apostle's good news of liberty in Jesus. As the testimonies throughout affirm, believers who have been frustrated and disillusioned by the failures of other strategies will find *new, true hope* here—in the crucified, risen, ruling Savior and His ever-present Spirit.

DENNIS E. JOHNSON, professor emeritus of practical theology, Westminster Seminary California

As a born-again believer and pastor of a church in Ireland, I have journeyed through the same battles as many who are reading this now. I know the difficulties many of us have in walking free from the desires that seek to have us walk in shame and self-condemnation. I believe John has opened an incredible resource, not only to individuals who have tried and failed so many times such that their hope has been stolen from their lives but also for parents and church leaders to have something tangible to help those they know find freedom. I want to thank John for taking hold of a subject so often avoided and opening our eyes to the true power of the gospel of Jesus Christ.

DAVID WILLIAMSON, senior pastor, Connections Church, Dublin, Republic of Ireland

This book is dedicated to a controversial topic: sexuality. Especially among Christians, there is no common position on this. So it is good when John Fonville takes a look at a central biblical text (1 Cor. 6:9–20) on the subject and presents his thoughtful and convincingly formulated interpretation. His interest in the gospel as the basis of Christian life in this world represents a new approach that deserves our attention.

ANDREAS STEGMANN, lecturer for church history at the Humboldt-Universität zu Berlin and director for German Reformation Studies at the Wittenberg Center for Reformation Studies

John Fonville clearly states his aim "to show that the gospel, not practical steps or more self-discipline, is God's provision for the power to live a life of purity, and it is available to every Christian." This he seeks to do by focusing on Paul's teaching in his letters to the Corinthians and by contrasting this with the total ineffectiveness of legalism and all other kinds of discipline and human effort. Emphasizing Paul's repeated use of the phrase "Do you not know . . . ?" the author shows how the power of the gospel is the only answer—not only to guilt and self-condemnation but also to corruption and slavery to sin. The prevalence of sexual sin in the world and in the church today is such that this book meets an urgent need and will be of great help to many.

BENJAMIN KWASHI, bishop of the Anglican Diocese of Jos and archbishop of the Ecclesiastical Province of Jos in the Church of Nigeria

In this lively, engaging, and thoughtful meditation on 1 Corinthians 6, John Fonville charts a map of the gospel-driven *sexual* life, a life moved by the gospel, shaped by God's moral law, and lived in union with Christ to whom we belong both body and soul.

R. Scott Clark, professor of church history and historical theology, Westminster Seminary California; president, Heidelberg Reformation Association

I cannot think of a more timely book than one that beautifully and persuasively considers the essential relationship between the gospel and the Christian's sexuality. John Fonville has been a close friend of mine for fifteen years now, and whenever I have wanted greater clarity on an issue's relationship to the gospel, he is the one I've called. He's never failed to provide me with the clarity I've needed. So, I am thrilled that everyone else can now benefit from John's gospel-saturated wisdom and insight as I have these many years.

Dan Cruver, resource manager at Desiring God; editor/coauthor of *Reclaiming Adoption*

This book is for the weary, the struggling, the Christian whose joy has been drained as a result of sexual brokenness. It is simple, yet profound, cutting right to the heart of godliness, particularly sexual holiness. It is discerningly countercultural, illustrating the dead end that society's morality will lead to with its emptiness and inadequacy. In this extended application of (principally) 1 Corinthians, it also runs contra a prevailing church culture that answers sexual brokenness either by changing its teaching (to accommodate) or burdening its members with new techniques to conquer sexual temptation. Both of these deny the gospel, and John Fonville, knowing both the gospel of God and the human heart, gently pastors the reader to know Christ, His love, grace, and acceptance, and to rejoice, living fully in it. This is a refreshingly different book, drawing on (among others) Calvin and Cranmer, and freshly written for this moment in a way we so desperately need. It needs to be shared widely so every Christian can drink from its deep well of gospel truth and refreshing grace. It gives me great pleasure to fulsomely commend its contents.

Trevor Johnston, senior pastor/rector, All Saints' Church, Belfast

Confronting the proverbial elephant in the evangelical room, John Fonville takes a fresh look at 1 Corinthians 6:9–20 to help Christians who struggle with sexual sin. In so doing, he eschews tired traditional exhortations to simply try harder at self-shaming and self-denial as the way to biblical purity. Instead, Fonville shows how the apostle Paul applied the law-gospel distinction to the rampant sexual immorality among the saints of God in Corinth. For while the law tells us how to live, only the gospel empowers us to do so. Consequently, Paul reminded his readers whom God had already made them to be in Christ. As a deeply experienced pastor, Fonville wisely does the same. He urges his readers to constantly remind themselves of that foundational gospel truth, which is the root of all Christian holiness: only God's love for sinners will inspire sinners to love God more than sin.

Ashley Null, Wittenberg Center for Reformation Studies

H

HOPE &

HOLINESS

HOW
THE GOSPEL
ENABLES
AND
EMPOWERS
SEXUAL
PURITY

JOHN
FONVILLE

MOODY PUBLISHERS
CHICAGO

This book is based on and contains adapted content from the author's sermon series "Do You Not Know?" (www.paramountchurch.com).

All names and details of personal anecdotes have been changed to protect individuals' privacy.

Emphasis to Scripture has been added by the author.

Published in association with the literary agency of Stan Guthrie Communications.

Edited by Pamela J. Pugh
Interior design: Ragont Design
Cover design: Erik M. Peterson

Library of Congress Cataloging-in-Publication Data

Names: Fonville, John (Rector), author.
Title: Hope and holiness : how the gospel enables and empowers sexual purity / John Fonville.
Description: Chicago : Moody Publishers, 2022. | Includes bibliographical references. | Summary: "Author John Fonville shows that the gospel is God's provision for the power to live a life of sexual purity. And it's available to every Christian. With a shepherding heart and theological acumen, Fonville sets us on a desperately needed joyful path of renewed strength and faith-filled purity"-- Provided by publisher.
Identifiers: LCCN 2022017580 (print) | LCCN 2022017581 (ebook) | ISBN 9780802428899 (paperback) | ISBN 9780802474971 (ebook)
Subjects: LCSH: Sex--Biblical teaching. | Bible. Corinthians, 1st, VI, 9-20--Criticism, interpretation, etc. | BISAC: RELIGION / Christian Living / Family & Relationships | RELIGION / Christian Ministry / Pastoral Resources
Classification: LCC BS2675.6.S36 F66 2022 (print) | LCC BS2675.6.S36 (ebook) | DDC 227/.206--dc23/eng/20220523
LC record available at https://lccn.loc.gov/2022017580
LC ebook record available at https://lccn.loc.gov/2022017581

Originally delivered by fleets of horse-drawn wagons, the affordable paperbacks from D. L. Moody's publishing house resourced the church and served everyday people. Now, after more than 125 years of publishing and ministry, Moody Publishers' mission remains the same—even if our delivery systems have changed a bit. For more information on other books (and resources) created from a biblical perspective, go to www.moodypublishers.com or write to

Moody Publishers
820 N. LaSalle Boulevard
Chicago, IL 60610

1 3 5 7 9 10 8 6 4 2

Printed in the United States of America

To Kathryn, who knew long before me
that Christ died for the sins of Christians, too.

CONTENTS

FOREWORD

"Do you not know ... ?"

As John Fonville points out, this is a recurring question in Paul's first letter to the Corinthians. The assumption is that they should have known, having been taught well the truths that shape their identity in Christ. However, in many ways Christians in Corinth were behaving as if they did not know that they were united to Christ: set apart (sanctified), justified, washed, and filled with the Holy Spirit.

A Roman colony, Corinth was known as something like the "Las Vegas" of the empire. With its flourishing cult of Aphrodite, the goddess of love, prostitution and homosexuality were normalized. Love was confused with lust. Yet, as Paul indicates and other historical sources substantiate, the city was full of greed, petty lawsuits, and oppression of the poor. What unites these vices is narcissism with its demand for instant gratification. The Corinthians lived consistently with their worldview. But in the Corinthian church, many were not living consistently with the worldview that they professed. "Do you not know ... ?"

Right at the outset of this disciplinary epistle, Paul reminds them of who they are in Christ. Strikingly, he does not excommunicate this disordered church. On the contrary, he addresses them as "those sanctified in Christ Jesus, called to be saints together with all those who in every place call upon the name of our Lord Jesus Christ, both their Lord and ours." He adds, "Grace to you and peace from God our Father and the Lord Jesus Christ" (1 Cor. 1:2–3). The apostle goes so far as to say, "I give thanks to my God always for you because of the grace that was given to you in Christ Jesus, that in every way you were enriched in him in all speech and all knowledge," assuring them that Christ "will sustain you to the end, guiltless in the day of our Lord Jesus Christ. God is faithful, by whom you were called into the fellowship of his Son, Jesus Christ our Lord" (vv. 4–5, 8–9).

As if this were not enough encouragement, he reminds them of the gospel he preached and upon which the church in Corinth and everywhere else is founded: "And because of him you are in Christ Jesus, who became to us wisdom from God, righteousness and sanctification and redemption" (v. 30). Indeed, while he was with them, he says, "I decided to know nothing among you except Jesus Christ and him crucified" (1 Cor. 2:2).

"Ah, yes, Paul, that's exactly why this church is a moral mess," one might expect to have heard from the apostle's detractors. "Too much preaching of grace leads to license. You need to tell them, right out of the gate, what you told the legalistic Galatians: they are on the verge of no longer even being a church."

Whether applied to individuals or to churches, it really matters what we say first. "Do you not know . . . ?" Paul was convinced that the Corinthian believers needed to go back to the gospel to discover who they are in Christ in order to realize the disconnect of truth from practice. That is the difference between natural virtue and saving grace. Union with Christ brings justification, sanctification, and, ultimately, glorification in an unbreakable chain of blessings. Paul doesn't want the church to be the moral police of Corinth, but to be a colony of Christ's heavenly kingdom in the middle of a godless society. "For what have I to do with judging outsiders? Is it not those inside the church whom you are to judge?" (1 Cor. 5:12).

Precisely because the church is holy in Christ, the unrepentant person who is infecting it with his flagrant sins must be disciplined. If he will not listen to the church's admonition, he must be cast out (v. 13).

But the church, apparently, was not even calling people to repentance. The disorder led the church to mirror its Corinthian environment: litigious, greedy, given to dissensions, divorce, and sexual immorality. Their worship was a mockery, with self-acclaimed "spiritual" Christians parading their tongues-speaking (without interpretation). It was more like *American Idol* than the edification of all, including unbelievers who, instead of glorifying God, conclude that they are "out of [their] minds" (1 Cor. 14:20–24). They were making a parody of the Lord's Supper, turning the sacrament of unity in Christ into another occasion to exhibit the socioeconomic divisions of society.

Does any of this sound familiar?

Focusing especially on Paul's indictment of sexual immorality in 1 Corinthians, John Fonville unpacks the indicative foundation (i.e., the gospel) and the imperatives that are the consistent outworking of our new life in Christ. In both moves, Fonville stays close to the biblical text with clear, logical, and beautifully persuasive arguments. His practical exhortations, even pastoral advice, are informed by years of ministry in and out of the pulpit. Instead of skimming the surface with "how-tos" that might come from any source or transforming the law and the gospel into therapeutic categories, he shows that the Word of God is powerful enough to do the job.

Especially powerful is the author's stress, following Paul, upon the body in Christian discipleship. We are not our own but were created in God's image and bought with a price. Honoring God with our bodies is a desperately needed emphasis in our day especially. There is an almost gnostic assumption that we can give our souls to Jesus and our bodies to false saviors and lords. We can follow Jesus in our heart, while giving our bodies to the daily tokens of the imperial cult. We may sing "In Christ Alone" one day and then return to pornography and other forms of self-indulgence the rest of the week.

But these false saviors and lords do not liberate; instead, they enslave us. Not freedom, but bondage; not autonomy, but powerlessness;

not self-respect, but self-loathing are the consequences of giving our bodies to someone or something other than our true Liberator. John Fonville explores richly the kindness of God that leads us to repentance. The reader will find here, as I have, a treasure of wisdom for that marvelous freedom that Christ purchased and wants us to enjoy.

—MICHAEL HORTON

THE GREAT DISCONNECT

THIS BOOK IS NOT ABOUT what we *know*. For example, we know that the West is saturated with sexual sin and brokenness. However, if you're unsure about this statement, there are plenty of data points to back it up. No one has to look far to find public displays and approving proclamations of immoral, even aberrant, behavior. Not only do we see this often in the entertainment industry but, within the church itself, many struggle or have even lost their way from following biblical standards.

For example, the Church of England states that sexual relations are for married heterosexual couples only—an undisputed teaching of Christendom for two millennia. Then, under withering social criticism, the archbishops of York and Canterbury apologize for the statement, which they say "jeopardised trust," adding, "We are very sorry and recognize the division and hurt this has caused."[1]

Gallup reports that 71 percent of Americans believe that heterosexual sex between consenting unmarried adults is morally acceptable, while 63 percent give a pass to gay or lesbian relations. Sex between teenagers, meanwhile, gets the go-ahead from 38 percent. Pornography is acceptable to 37 percent, polygamy to 18 percent. In a slender ray of good news, only 9 percent approve of married men and women having an affair.[2]

Tragically, we also know that this sexual sickness has infected the church—with a vengeance. A recent survey by the Pew Research Center found that 46 percent of evangelicals in the United States are okay with premarital sex in a committed relationship.[3] According to Barna Research, 57 percent of pastors and 64 percent of youth pastors "admit they have struggled with porn, either currently or in the past. Overall, 21 percent of youth pastors and 14 percent of pastors admit they currently struggle with using porn."[4]

Meanwhile, 41 percent of Christian men aged thirteen to twenty-four say they "frequently" use porn. For Christian men aged twenty-five and older, it's a robust 23 percent. These discouraging numbers come despite the fact that a super majority of Americans view pornography as wrong and that one study after another shows its linkage to depression, decreased brain function, the objectification of women's bodies, less happiness for women in relationships with men who consumed it in childhood, and a lessened ability in men who used it in an attempt to form healthy relationships.[5]

As writer Halee Gray Scott notes, "Porn isn't just an individual moral problem. It strikes to the heart of what it means to be human."[6] And Christians—even pastors—who should know better seem to be just as susceptible to becoming ensnared.

Moreover, we know all too well that rarely a month goes by without a report of a high-profile Christian being credibly accused of sexual misconduct. Some resign their positions in disgrace; others are forced out; a few doggedly hang on to their ministries, brazen and unfazed. While the divorce rates among Christians who attend church regularly are less than those of their unchurched neighbors, we're not all that different in our response to sexual temptation.

Frankly, it's getting harder and harder to feel surprise when a prominent, well-thought-of person announces that he is leaving his wife for someone else who "makes him happy." C. S. Lewis saw all this coming when he told the story of "Mr. A.," who deserted his wife of many years for "Mrs. B." "Mrs. A.," according to Lewis, may have "consumed herself by bearing his children and nursing him through the long illness that overshadowed their earlier married life." Lewis added drily, "You mustn't, by the way, imagine that A. was the sort of man who nonchalantly threw a wife away like the peel of an orange he'd sucked dry. Her suicide was a terrible shock to him. We all knew this, for he told us so himself. 'But what could I do?' he said. 'A man has a right to happiness. I had to take my one chance when it came.'"[7]

Somehow, there is a great disconnect for Christians between our professions about sex when we declare that relations must take place only between a married man and woman, and our practice. Why aren't we doing better? We know it's not for lack of resources. We have shelves full of books extolling the benefits and satisfaction of sex in marriage, if any prudes among us remain. Then there are the many Christian resources on recovering from sexual addiction and related issues. Multitudes of organizations are devoted to purity—physical, emotional, and mental.

We have been given endless rules, vows, software filters, accountability talks and groups, exemplary challenges to be like Joseph or not be like Samson (a he-man with a she-weakness, as he is often portrayed). Or you are told to pop a rubber band on your wrist every time you have an impure thought. On and on the list goes.

No matter how "spiritual" these approaches may appear, I contend that they actually promote confidence in self rather than confidence in Christ—not to mention they are useless on their own. In Colossians 2:23 Paul writes, "These have indeed an appearance of wisdom in promoting self-made religion and asceticism and severity to the body, but they are of no value in stopping the indulgence of the flesh."

As a pastor I see a lot of this in a local church setting. I once received an email from a friend who struggled with sexual temptation. Well-meaning Christians had advised him on steps he could take, anything from finding an accountability buddy to working out at the gym when tempted. My friend said that while the advice was good, there was no power in any of it.

I agree with him. But pointing out that these approaches are powerless to change us is not the same thing as saying that we must *remain* powerless. There *is* hope. There *is* a solution. It's not a technique, a discipline, or a cliché. It's the power of God, which is what we must know.

What is that power? What is it that we must know but do not know, at least as well as we should? The apostle Paul reveals the answer. "For I am not ashamed of the gospel," he says in the first portion of Romans 1:16, "for it is the power of God for salvation to everyone who believes." *The gospel is what we must know because the gospel provides all the power we need.* "The power of God for salvation"—yes, this includes the wonderful promise of the salvation of our souls and bodies in the resurrection. But the salvation brought by the gospel—the good news that Christ's life, death, burial, and resurrection have opened the door to paradise to all who repent and receive Him by faith alone—also includes the promise of our minds and bodies being redeemed and renewed. We don't have to wait for this salvation. Eternal life begins right now.

> **The aim of this book is to show that the gospel, not practical steps or more self-discipline, is God's provision for the power to live a life of purity, and it is available to every Christian.**

As 2 Corinthians 5:17 declares, "Therefore, if anyone is in Christ, he is a new creation. The old has passed away; behold, the new has come." As new creations, disciples of Christ are no longer at the mercy of old temptations, lusts, and lies. We are truly free . . . if we want to be. The New Testament teaches this truth over and over. Our biggest problem is that we have failed to believe and appropriate it. We don't know the gospel as we should.

The aim of this book is to show that the gospel, not practical steps or more self-discipline, is God's provision for the power to live a life of purity, and it is available to every Christian.

This book is an extended reflection on how to keep the seventh commandment. As Christians, we are called to obey the seventh commandment, namely, "You shall not commit adultery" (Ex. 20:14). It is God's will that believers abstain from all sexual immorality and live chaste and pure lives, whether in marriage or single life (1 Cor. 6:9–20; Eph. 5:3–5; Heb. 13:4). Because our body and soul are both temples of the Holy Spirit, it is God's will that we keep both pure and holy. This is why God, in His law, forbids everything that incites unchastity, whether it be actions, looks, talk, thoughts, or desires.[8]

However, it is not enough to know *what* God's law forbids and requires. We must also know *how* to actually keep God's law. Thus, the central claim of this book is this: *Only the gospel can empower obedience to God's law.*[9] The gospel provides a double blessing: the forgiveness of sin and the power for holiness.[10] The gospel gives what the law requires, which in this instance is to abstain from all sexual immorality and live sexually pure lives whether in marriage or single life.

And so, we'll attempt to make the case for gospel power and purity over sexual sin by thoroughly examining an absolutely vital question that Paul repeatedly asked another group of Christians mired in sexual sin—the church in ancient Corinth: Do you not know? We find this interrogative throughout 1 Corinthians 6:9–20:

> *Or do you not know that the unrighteous will not inherit the kingdom of God?* Do not be deceived: neither the sexually immoral, nor idolaters, nor adulterers, nor men who practice homosexuality, nor thieves, nor the greedy, nor

drunkards, nor revilers, nor swindlers will inherit the kingdom of God. And such were some of you. But you were washed, you were sanctified, you were justified in the name of the Lord Jesus Christ and by the Spirit of our God. "All things are lawful for me," but not all things are helpful. "All things are lawful for me," but I will not be dominated by anything. "Food is meant for the stomach and the stomach for food"—and God will destroy both one and the other. The body is not meant for sexual immorality, but for the Lord, and the Lord for the body. And God raised the Lord and will also raise us up by his power. *Do you not know that your bodies are members of Christ?* Shall I then take the members of Christ and make them members of a prostitute? Never! Or *do you not know that he who is joined to a prostitute becomes one body with her?* For, as it is written, "The two will become one flesh." But he who is joined to the Lord becomes one spirit with him. Flee from sexual immorality. Every other sin a person commits is outside the body, but the sexually immoral person sins against his own body. Or *do you not know that your body is a temple of the Holy Spirit within you, whom you have from God? You are not your own*, for you were bought with a price. So glorify God in your body.

Paul's question, and the life-affirming answers that flow from it, will occupy the balance of this volume. "Do you not know . . . ?"

Part 1

Who Are We?

1 CORINTHIANS 6:9–11

Chapter 1

DO WE KNOW THE GOSPEL?

"MY HUSBAND AND I lived a lie in our relationship and marriage for almost ten years," a woman confessed to me after a church service. "On the outside, we were a happy couple, so in love, in sync, playful, serving our church and those around us. However, behind closed doors and in our hearts, we were failing miserably. Our marriage was incredibly rocky. I lived in a constant state of anxiety: Is he going to act out while I'm at work? Is this my fault?"

The problems were not due to a lack of trying on her part. Trisha told me, "When we were dating, I thought, 'Surely when we get married, he won't have these sexual issues.' When that turned out not to be true, I thought, 'Surely when we have kids, he won't have these sexual issues.' That didn't happen either. I kept hoping and praying things would change. I tried yelling, pleading, threatening, shaming, crying, shutting him out, anything and everything I could think of to force him to stop. Nothing helped."

Her experience mirrors that of many sincere Christians who are faced with sexual addiction and sin. No matter what they do, they cannot escape it in their own power, or free others from its grip.

It is an old story—as old as the Christian church. The apostle Paul dealt with it in Corinth, a city steeped in sexual immorality. But unlike

23

so many Christians in our day, Paul knew that the answer was not to try harder, to yell, shut out, or shame. It was to apply the good news of Jesus Christ to our hearts. Only through the gospel could hearts be truly changed, leading to changed behavior. The gospel is still the only way.

Before we delve into Paul's remarkable question to a church enslaved to sexual sin, let's look at four foundational truths about sex.[1]

1. WE ARE MADE IN THE IMAGE OF GOD

First, in terms of human nature, the Bible doesn't begin with the fall and the doctrine of total depravity. If it did, rather than with God's good creation, we could easily assume that human beings are simply rotten from the beginning, void of any goodness and intrinsic dignity.[2] The Bible, however, begins by setting forth the *goodness* of God's creation (Gen. 1). From the beginning God declared His creation to be "very good" (Gen. 1:31).

This means that human beings—pre-fall—were created basically good in their intrinsic nature, endowed with free will, beauty of body and soul, reason, and moral excellence. Simply put, human beings are made in the image of God.

Even after the fall, mankind still retains the image of God, although it is now greatly obscured and marred by sin. German Reformed theologian Zacharias Ursinus (1534–1583) writes, "The vestiges and remains of the image of God in man, although they are greatly obscured and marred by sin, are, nevertheless, still preserved in us to a certain extent."[3] Therefore, all of us possess an intrinsic dignity. This has important implications for human sexuality.

Accordingly, there is no place for discrimination or dehumanizing of an individual who is trapped in any form of extramarital, aberrant sexual sin (or any type of sin!).[4] Uncharitable statements about those ensnared by sin are unchristian and ought to be condemned by every Christian, including Christian leaders.

All human beings are image bearers of God. This demands respect for all human life, Christian or not. Michael Horton writes, "Only in Christ do we realize the salvation and the goal of our personhood by the gospel, but the law that binds us to our neighbors and co-bearers of God's image obliges us to treat them as persons."[5]

Jesus treats the woman "caught in the act of adultery" with utmost dignity while confronting her illicit behavior (John 8:4). One can only imagine the shame, embarrassment, and fear that gripped this woman as her accusers dragged her before Jesus to be stoned. But this is not how Jesus deals with sinners. Jesus is not a new Moses, who demanded "Do this and live." Rather, He is the Mediator of a new and better covenant (Heb. 8:6; 12:24).[6]

Horton writes, "When Jesus inaugurated the Lord's Supper in the upper room, He declared, 'This is my blood of the covenant, which is poured out for many for the forgiveness of sins' (Matt. 26:28). Instead of a covenant of law ('Do this and you shall live'), it is a covenant of free mercy. Unlike Moses, He did not dash the blood on the people, confirming their oath, but pledged His oath in His own blood. He alone passed between the pieces, bearing the judgment in our place."[7]

In John 3:17, Jesus says of the Father, "For God did not send his Son into the world to condemn the world, but in order that the world might be saved through him." As One who is a friend of tax collectors and sinners, Jesus says to the woman, "'Woman, where are they? Has no one condemned you?' She said, 'No one, Lord.' And Jesus said, 'Neither do I condemn you; go, and from now on sin no more'" (John 8:10–11). Though guilty of adultery, this woman is treated with dignity and respect by Jesus. Her adulterous sin cut to the very fabric of her personhood. She was a fallen, broken child of Adam who needed grace in order to be adopted as a child of God.

John Stott observes that talk about our sexuality touches a point close to the center of our personality.[8] When we talk about human sexuality, a vital part of our identity is being discussed—and perhaps endorsed or threatened. Therefore, let's remember that whatever inclination or struggle a person may experience in this area, all people are made in the image of God and are worthy of respect and dignity.

2. WE ARE SEXUAL BEINGS

Our bodies as well as our sexuality are basic to our humanity. God created both. God created us as physical beings: "The LORD God formed the man of dust from the ground and breathed into his nostrils the breath of life, and the man became a living creature" (Gen. 2:7). God also created sexuality. He made mankind male and female: "So God created man in his own image, in the image of God he created him; male and female he created them" (Gen. 1:27). Thus, we are not disembodied, sexless beings like angels. Because our bodies and sexuality are basic to our humanness, the desires for sensual pleasure are not bad and do not indicate a weakness or defect in human nature. Rather, the desires of the body for sensual pleasure indicate what it is to experience human nature as God created it.

During the Reformation, John Calvin criticized Roman Catholic theology for locating sin in an alleged weakness of human nature itself. Horton explains,

> According to this view, human beings are related to God and the angels by virtue of their "higher self"—the mind or soul—but are related to other animals by virtue of their "lower self"—the appetites associated with the body. This idea, influenced by Plato, gave rise to the notion of *concupiscence*: that is, the desires of the body for sensual pleasure. Concupiscence [author note: according to Thomas Aquinas] is not itself sin until it is acted upon, but it does suggest a weakness or defect in human nature as created by God. Aquinas, following Augustine, spoke of this concupiscence as the "kindling wood" for the fire of passion that leads to actual sins.[9]

Because of this wrong view of human nature, married life was considered a lower—though not evil—form of life in contrast to the contemplative life of the monk. Sexual relations within marriage were said to be for procreative purposes only and not for sensual pleasure. Horton explains, "It is this sensual (animal) aspect of our constitution that drags us down from the heights of pure spiritual contemplation."[10] Calvin rightly rejected this body-soul dualism that identified sin with the body. Nowhere do the Scriptures teach that concupiscence (i.e., sinful inclination; original sin and the seedbed of sin)[11] is in any way due to a weakness of nature (i.e., the body and its desires). Thus, Horton concludes,

> The most fundamental problem with this view, says Calvin, is that it attributes sin to human nature as God created it. Against those "who dare write God's name upon their own faults," Calvin says, "they perversely search out God's handiwork in their own pollution, when they ought rather to have sought it in that unimpaired and uncorrupted nature of Adam." Not God, but we are guilty "solely because we have degenerated from our original condition." Our mortal wound comes not from nature itself, but from its corruption through the fall.[12]

This leads us to a third introductory comment.

3. WE ARE ALL SEXUAL SINNERS

Because of the fall—rather than a weakness or defect in human nature as created by God—our bodies, as well as our minds, hearts, and wills are all under the enslavement of sin and death. Every part of our being has been infected with sin, including our sexuality. And even though we are not as bad as we possibly could be, we are radically and equally corrupt, impure, and guilty before God. Horton writes, "We are all guilty and corrupt to such an extent that there is no hope of pulling ourselves together, brushing ourselves off, and striving (with the help of grace) to overcome God's judgment and our own rebellion."[13]

Ecclesiastes 7:20 states, "Surely there is not a righteous man on earth who does good and never sins." In Romans 3 Paul writes,

> All, both Jews and Greeks, are under sin, as it is written: "None is righteous, no, not one; no one understands; no one seeks for God. All have turned aside; together they have become worthless; no one does good, not even one." . . . we know that whatever the law says it speaks to those who are under the law, so that every mouth may be stopped, and the whole world may be held accountable to God. . . . all have sinned and fall short of the glory of God. (Rom. 3:9–12, 19, 23; cf. Isa. 53:6)

No one is sexually sinless. No one can claim to have fulfilled God's ideal for sexual purity. Jesus said it like this: "You have heard that it was said, 'You shall not commit adultery.' But I say to you that everyone who looks at a woman with lustful intent has already committed adultery with her in his heart" (Matt. 5:27–28). Only Jesus lived a sexually sinless life in thought, desire, and deed.

As Stott writes, "We are frail and vulnerable. We are pilgrims on our way to God. We are very far from having arrived. We are engaged in an unremitting conflict with the world, the flesh, and the devil. . . . Because all of us are sinners, we all stand under the judgment of God, and we are all in urgent need of the grace of God. Besides, sexual sins are not the only sins, nor even necessarily the most sinful; pride and hypocrisy are surely worse."[14]

To suggest that sexual sin is not the only sin (or even the primary sin) is not to imply that sexual sin is not a serious problem with disastrous consequences. Sexual sin can have devastating effects on individuals, marriages, families, and society as a whole. But sex and sensual physical desire are not the problem. The problem is that we are fallen; all of us sexual sinners!

> **Sexual immorality slices deep into our personhood. It causes frustration, guilt, hurt, and shame.**

But if sexual sin is not the primary sin—the worst sin—why does Paul devote two chapters to it in 1 Corinthians? Why does he address it so often? Why is it the first item in Paul's vice lists?[15]

The reason is twofold: First, as the Corinthians were discovering, gaining freedom from this idol is difficult.

Second, sexual immorality can provoke deep shame, hopelessness, and huge amounts of guilt in people who struggle with this enslaving sin. Sexual immorality slices deep into our personhood. It causes frustration, guilt, hurt, and shame. Such a fallen, broken state demands an enormous amount of concrete, specific gospel truth and application.

So, before we continue, I think it's vital to emphasize the following point:

There is no condemnation for Christians who **struggle** *with sexual sin and sinful desires.*

This may strike you as surprising, but it is true (see 1 Cor. 6:11). Question 60 in the Heidelberg Catechism asks, "How are you righteous before God?" Here's the comforting answer (emphasis added):

> Only by true faith in Jesus Christ; that is, *although my conscience accuses me that I have grievously sinned against all the commandments of God, have never kept any of them, and that I am still prone always to all evil,* yet God, without any merit of mine, of mere grace, grants and imputes to me the perfect

satisfaction, righteousness and holiness of Christ, as if I had never committed nor had any sins, and had myself accomplished all the obedience which Christ has fulfilled for me, if only I accept such benefit with a believing heart.[16]

In Galatians 5:17, Paul recognizes that the Christian life is a struggle—an unremitting conflict between the flesh and the Spirit: "For the desires of the flesh are against the Spirit, and the desires of the Spirit are against the flesh, for these are opposed to each other, to keep you from doing the things you want to do." Such a continuous struggle indicates our continual need for the gospel. Tim Chester writes,

> Alongside your talk about sex needs to go talk about grace. And not just grace in the abstract, but the grace of God in the death of Christ. Christ dies in our place, bearing our guilt so that there is now no condemnation for those who are in Christ Jesus. . . . There is no condemnation for porn users, adulterers, sexual fantasists who are in Christ Jesus. This is not being soft on sin. Quite the opposite. It takes sin seriously, so seriously that the only remedy is the death of the eternal Son of God. . . . Churches are full of people desperately trying to self-atone for their lust, desperately trying to sort themselves out, desperately trying to prove they are good enough for God. Our message must be, "It is finished. Christ has done it all."[17]

The good news is that the desires of our flesh do not have the final say. Though at times it may feel like the desires of your flesh will prevail, they won't! For the Christian, the desires of the flesh will not and cannot win. In Galatians 5:24, Paul writes, "Those who belong to Christ Jesus have crucified the flesh with its passions and desires." This is good news in the believer's daily battle with the flesh!

Now, you may be wondering, "When did I crucify the passions and desires of my flesh?" The answer is found in the word "crucified." John Calvin writes,

> The word *crucified* is employed to point out that the mortification of the flesh is the effect of the cross of Christ. This work does not belong to man. By the grace of Christ "we have been planted together in the likeness of his death" (Rom. 6:5) that we no longer might live unto ourselves.[18]

The crucifixion of the passions and desires of our flesh took place at conversion when the Holy Spirit by grace alone through faith alone united us to Christ in His death. Because believers "belong to Christ" (i.e., are united with Christ), they share in His death and thus the desires of the flesh have been forever defeated!

Take heart, struggling believer! You are no longer a slave to the desires of the flesh. You are now a free man or woman!

So then, take heart, struggling believer! The gospel announces that you are not left powerless to the ruling and reigning desires of the flesh. You are no longer a slave. You are now a free man or woman! Because all believers now share in Christ's death, they are no longer enslaved to the desires of the flesh.

To be sure, this verse doesn't imply perfection (i.e., no longer experiencing the warring opposition of the flesh). Neither Romans 6 nor Galatians 5 teaches a sinless perfection (Gal. 5:17; Rom. 7:14–23). Rather, the point is that the power of sin has been broken in those who believe. John Calvin writes, "The flesh is not yet indeed entirely destroyed; but it has no right to exercise dominion, and ought to yield to the Spirit."[19]

We will see in chapter 2 that Christians will still experience a mighty struggle with the flesh, but the desires of the flesh no longer rule and reign in us. Paul is announcing that Jesus' victorious death is also ours! Consequently, by virtue of our union with Christ, we are now free to walk by the Spirit and triumph—albeit imperfectly—over the desires of the flesh, which formerly dominated us. The Holy Spirit, who is better than any external law, will produce a life that is pleasing to God in every respect. This leads us to one final, introductory, clarifying comment:

4. WE ARE ALL DEFICIENT IN OUR KNOWLEDGE OF THE GOSPEL AND ITS IMPLICATIONS FOR OUR LIVES

A great eighteenth-century Scottish preacher, Ralph Erskine, wrote, "They that think they know the Gospel well enough bewray [reveal] their ignorance; no man can be too evangelical, it will take all his lifetime to get a legal temper [disposition] destroyed."[20] The fact is, we really do not know the gospel and its implications for our lives as well as we should. The law is a doctrine whose seed is written by nature in our hearts. In contrast, the gospel is a doctrine that is not at all in us by nature, but which is revealed from heaven (Matt. 16:17; John 1:13) and totally surpasses natural knowledge.[21]

So it should not surprise us that in 1 Corinthians Paul asks the all-important question, "Do you not know?" ten times (six occur in chapter 6).[22] In each instance, Paul's question is intended to draw the Corinthians' attention to a cardinal truth of the Christian faith—one that ought to be self-evident and unavoidable. In 1 Corinthians 6, Paul's question is intended to draw the Corinthians' attention to the paramount truth of the Christian faith (see 1 Cor. 15:3), namely the gospel and its implications for their sexuality. But the Corinthian believers didn't really know the gospel and its implications, particularly concerning sexual immorality. This shouldn't have escaped the Corinthians' thinking—and it must not escape *our* thinking.

However, since it *did* escape their thinking, Paul appeals to specific gospel truths and the fruit of the gospel as the remedy for the Corinthians' sexual immorality. We will come to see how Paul appeals to the doctrines of regeneration, sanctification, justification, adoption, resurrection, union with Christ, redemption, and the gift of the Spirit. This certainly puts to rest any notion that doctrine isn't practical!

Paul's concern in chapter 6—in fact, in the whole book—is to set forth a gospel-centered vision of community in the church. Throughout his arguments in 1 Corinthians, Paul is not only concerned for the welfare of the individual but also for the welfare of the community of believers—the church.[23] The failure of the Corinthian church to act in gospel-centered ways damaged the church's unity and witness to the world. And so, Paul, in chapter 5, calls on the Corinthian believers to discipline—rather than arrogantly tolerate—a man in the church involved in an incestuous relationship. We must never be among those who think the gospel and God's grace wink at sin. Craig Blomberg writes,

> Such people fail to grasp God's utter repugnance to sin and his infinitely perfect standards for holiness. Further, we must avoid a cheap grace that refuses to force professing believers to face up to the destructive consequences of grossly immoral behavior. They are not only damaging themselves by allowing sin to go unchecked but also destroying the church.[24]

Paul then is addressing the failure of the church to *be* the church, for its members to be who they really are in Christ.[25] The ways of the world—their pagan past—have infiltrated and replaced the centrality of the gospel and its ethical implications for the church's life and ministry. Gordon Fee writes, "The gospel itself is at stake, not simply the resolution of an ethical question."[26]

At the end of each chapter in this book, I will share some theological reflections that will help readers apply its insights. Here are the first two:

REFLECTION

1. All the problems and imperfections that we experience are failures to be conformed to the gospel.
Anglican theologian Graeme Goldsworthy writes,

> As we begin the Christian life by placing our whole trust in the Christ of the gospel event, so in the same way we continue in the Christian life. The gospel not only brings us to the new birth and faith as Christians; it is God's means of saving us totally. The gospel is the power of God for salvation (Rom. 1:16), and this means the whole of salvation for the whole person. Thus the gospel converts us, the gospel sustains us in the Christian life and brings us to maturity and the gospel brings us to perfection through our resurrection from the dead. . . . All the problems and imperfections that we experience are failures to be conformed to the gospel. The only remedy that the New Testament prescribes for our problems is to bring our lives to conform to the gospel.[27]

The believers in Corinth were messed up theologically and morally. First Corinthians shows their pride and factionalism. They were suing one another and tolerating gross sexual immorality (apparently justifying it using theological arguments, e.g., 6:12–13). Abusing their freedom in Christ to an extreme, they corrupted the Lord's Supper, misused spiritual gifts, and lacked love. And they were utterly con-fused about the doctrine of resurrection—the hope of the gospel. In each case, Paul's strategy was to point them back to the gospel and its implications for Christian communities. Only the gospel can bring the believer's life into conformity with what the law requires—in this context, sexual purity.

In dealing with sexual immorality, Paul calls on the Corinthians to know the gospel and its implications. He wants them to know who they are after trusting in Christ and to act in accordance with their new identity as citizens of the kingdom of God ("saints," 1 Cor. 6:1–2). Their fundamental problem was failing to be conformed to the gospel and then live out its implications daily. They didn't know who they really were. They had a crisis of identity! And often, so do we.

2. We must never assume that we know the gospel and its full im-plications for our lives.

We really don't know the gospel and its implications for our lives as well as we should. The gospel and its life implications are not truths that come to us naturally. They are not self-evident. In fact, "the gospel is so odd, so against the grain of our natural inclinations, and the in-fatuations of our culture that nothing less than a miracle is required in order for there to be a true hearing."[28]

Instead of seeking to bring their lives into conformity with the gospel and its ethical implications, the Corinthians were being influ-enced by their pagan pasts. But Paul calls on them to live lives com-mensurate with their new status as citizens of the kingdom of God. Paul's million-dollar question "Do you not know?" highlights the incongruity between who the Corinthians are and how they are living.

Paul doesn't adopt ascetic, moralistic, or exemplary arguments to motivate the Corinthians to morally pure lives. Instead, he redi-rects them to the gospel and its implications. There's no list of "how to" steps for moral purity. How interesting, then, that "how to" lists are frequently the remedy offered to those struggling with sexual sin today, as the friend I mentioned in the introduction learned.

"Do you not know?" is the question that shines a searchlight on our real problem. What we don't know as evidenced by this letter and driven home by the rest of Scripture is that good news is the key to moral purity. There truly is no other way.

Chapter 2

WHY DO CHRISTIANS STRUGGLE?

GROWING UP IN A churchgoing family, Kate had been taught that maintaining her sexual purity for marriage was of "utmost importance." She had been taught many rules and regulations, but without being given any reasons for them. For example, having sex outside of marriage was a sin, but she didn't really know why, and she got little help from her mom and dad either by teaching or example. Though both parents were active in the church and the family was expected to attend faithfully and get involved, life at home was a different story. The parents' marriage was falling apart. Kate's father drifted away from the church and eventually left his family.

Entering puberty and the middle school years, Kate's interest in sex was growing through what she saw on television, discussions with her friends, and her own natural curiosity. "Often," Kate said later, "I felt ashamed and unsure what to do with these thoughts except to push them aside and move on. I was so sure they were sinful."

As she entered high school, those normal thoughts and desires turned into temptations. "I was ridden with feelings of guilt and overwhelmed by the memories of the 'purity culture' I grew up in," Kate recalled. "At times, I was ashamed to even like a boy or think he was attractive, because my legalistic background told me that this was sinful."

Eventually, however, Kate yielded "almost daily" to both fornication and an addiction to pornography. Such habitual sins made her doubt her salvation and left her feeling isolated from her sisters, who seemingly didn't struggle with such things. Throughout her teenage years and into her early twenties, she vacillated between living a life of godliness and falling back into sin. She pressured herself, made vows, and prayed, repeatedly asking God to make her obedient and rid her of sexual sin. All to no avail. Human effort in a moral cause was not enough.

"As hard as we try, we are broken human beings who will continue to fall over and over again throughout our lives," Kate now says. "We cannot depend on our obedience to God to save us from ourselves because we are inherently disobedient, sinful humans."

Slowly, Kate was coming to the realization that the answer to her sexual struggles was not in herself, but in someone—Someone—else. She moved to a gospel-centered church and began unlearning the legalistic lessons of her youth, replacing them with a new understanding of the gospel to transform her from the inside out.

"I began to see from my own life," Kate says, "that we are utterly incapable of obedience without the Holy Spirit's lovingkindness changing our hearts. Hearing the good news of the gospel every week was critical to my journey of overcoming habitual sexual sin. I left church each week remembering that Christ lived a sinless life, suffered death, was buried, and rose from the grave for my sexual immorality. I left accepting that I was a broken human and was going to sin, but that His grace had already covered my sins past, present, and future. I left knowing I was freed from the slavery of sin and was free to live my life as best as I could with the strength of the Lord in me."

It is often said, "It's not what you know that can hurt you; it's what you don't." Kate didn't know the key to sexual freedom and as a result lived in sexual bondage for many years. She is far from the first Christian to do so. Enter the Corinthians, who were a theological and moral mess. In 1 Corinthians 6:9–20, Paul reveals that their problem is that they didn't really know the gospel and its implications for their sexual behavior. As we said, Paul asks "Do you not know?" ten times in this letter, four of which appear in the passage we are studying in this book (1 Cor. 6:9, 15, 16, 19).

On the one hand, Paul's questioning serves as a rebuke and reveals his intensity of feeling. His questions in 1 Corinthians 6:9–20 are intended to draw the Corinthians' attention to the gospel and its implications for living a morally pure life that should have been self-evident and unavoidable.

But since this wasn't the case, Paul reintroduces the gospel as the remedy. Paul's *heavy* emphasis on the gospel must not be understood as an *exclusive* emphasis, thus neglecting the role of the law. In chapter 6, verse 9, Paul issues a strong warning against all who are characterized by serial, unrepentant sinning, asking, "Or do you not know that the unrighteous will not inherit the kingdom of God?" Those who live in open rebellion against God's law and have no inward desire to follow God's moral requirements have never tasted of the gospel! Question 90 in the Heidelberg Catechism asks, "What is the coming-to-life of the new self?" Here's the answer: "It is wholehearted joy in God through Christ; and a delight to do every kind of good as God wants us to."[1]

In addition to his warning, the apostle issues three strong imperatives: "do not be deceived," *mē planasthe* (v. 9), "flee," *pheugete* (v. 18), and "glorify," *doxasate* (v. 20). These are imperatives, not suggestions!

Paul has woven together a tapestry of law and gospel, because his pastoral strategy for liberating a heart from deep and complex enslavement to sexual sin is through the wise application of both the law (to warn and direct) and the gospel (to refocus and empower one's heart). *But as Paul weaves together a tapestry of law and gospel in chapter 6, he unloads a Mount Everest of gospel truth, which serves as the basis for all the imperatives in verses 9–20!*

How quickly we forget that *only the gospel gives what the law demands.* The problem with so many approaches to helping believers in this area is that they are almost exclusively law based. And to further complicate the problem, the "laws" that are given are not *God's* laws—as Paul gives in chapter 6—but rather constitute helpful advice, presented as "relevant and practical." But a diet of "relevant and practical" advice only imposes further expectations and demands as conditions for success.[2] When we fail to live up to these newly imposed expectations and conditions, we fall further into despair. Thus, we come to believe that while the law cannot justify us, it can sanctify us.[3]

> **Fallen hearts think that the role of religion is to give people moral instruction to keep us from being dominated by our sinful habits.**

Even if the law and gospel are carefully distinguished in justification, they are usually immediately confused in sanctification—the work of God's free grace, whereby we are renewed in the whole man after the image of God, and are enabled more and more to die unto sin, and live unto righteousness.[4] But the law can do no more in sanctification than it could in justification. We cannot find strength in the law to finish our journey any more than we could find strength in the law to begin our journey (see Gal. 3:3). Both pre-salvation and post-salvation, the basic function of the law never changes, which is to command.[5]

So, whether the law serves as a pedagogue to drive us to Christ or as a moral guide to direct our gratitude, it only commands and does nothing else.

Michael Horton writes, "The law can tell us what our gracious Father calls us to do, but it can never animate our hearts or motivate our hands" to do it.[6] Only the gospel is the power of God for salvation (i.e., God's means of saving us totally). This is what the Corinthians didn't know—what they had lost sight of—and it is what *we* do not know. The gospel way of holiness is not self-evident. Fallen hearts think that the role of religion is to give people moral instruction to keep us from being dominated by our sinful habits.[7]

But Paul reminds the Corinthians that the gospel is the answer not only to their guilt and condemnation but also to their corruption and slavery to sin. Anglican cleric Augustus Toplady (1740–1778) spoke of the gospel as "the double cure," saving us from both sin's guilt and its power.[8] As I stated in the introduction of this book: *Only the gospel can empower obedience to God's law*, which in this instance is to abstain from all sexual immorality and live sexually pure lives whether in marriage or singleness. Here in 1 Corinthians 6:9–20, Paul will argue that the gospel applies not only to the forgiveness of sin but also to a total transformation, beginning with regeneration, which gives us a new identity and leads to new obedience.

> **Christ, through the gospel, doesn't give us a mere moral makeover. He gives us a whole new identity.**

The author of *Chaos and Grace: Discovering the Liberating Work of the Holy Spirit* notes the undeniable fact that many religions, self-help and self-improvement programs, and therapies *work* . . . to a certain extent. These programs "enable people to break addictions, control tempers, repair relationships, and even practice forgiveness. Many social reform groups serve their neighbor."

But ultimately these approaches exhort people to become what they are *not*, making true and lasting change impossible. Behavior modification cannot transform a person's heart. Yet there is hope. "The Good News drills down deeper than this."⁹ Christ, through the gospel, doesn't give us a mere moral makeover. He gives us a whole new identity, one that comes through death and resurrection. Through the gospel, our sin is forgiven (justification), and we are empowered to live unto God (sanctification). As Ezekiel prophesied,

> "I will sprinkle clean water on you, and you shall be clean from all your uncleannesses, and from all your idols I will cleanse you. And I will give you a new heart, and a new spirit I will put within you. And I will remove the heart of stone from your flesh and give you a heart of flesh. And I will put my Spirit within you, and cause you to walk in my statutes and be careful to obey my rules." (Ezek. 36:25–27)

The point, then, is this: the only source of life and power for living the Christian life is the gospel—and this is what the Corinthians didn't know. Their ethical failures stemmed from a fundamental problem: they didn't know who they really were in Christ. They were suffering from an identity crisis! David Prior writes, "For all their so-called knowledge, the Christians at Corinth had lost sight of the centrality of Jesus Christ, the controlling power of the Holy Spirit and the transforming experience of having been called and saved by God."¹⁰ Paul knew that what the Corinthians needed wasn't moral pep talks to try harder or be better. No! He knew that the Corinthians needed a fresh knowledge of the gospel and its daily implications.

Therefore, in 1 Corinthians 6:9–20, Paul asks them four questions, beginning each time with, "Do you not know . . . ?" These four questions will reintroduce the Corinthians to the gospel and its implications, which alone produce obedience and holiness. Paul is calling on the Corinthians to know who they are in Christ—to see themselves as "saints" (1 Cor. 1:2; 6:1–2, 11)—and then to act in accordance with their new identity. *Paul is exhorting the Corinthians (and us!): "Become what you are."* Let me paraphrase what Paul is saying to the immoral Corinthians:

> You were serially sexually immoral, idolaters, adulterers, men who practice homosexuality, thieves, greedy, drunkards, revilers, and swindlers. But you are no longer these things. Now you are saints! So stop living and behaving like what you were. You have been washed, sanctified, and justified. You have a completely new identity. You are now saints; citizens of God's kingdom. Therefore, be who you are!

This is the gospel way of teaching holiness. Any other approach or remedy that is not presented in this way is neither scriptural nor Christian.

Now you may be thinking, "How could Paul call the Corinthians—who were a theological and moral mess—*saints*? I thought a saint is someone who has lived an exceptionally holy life and therefore is worthy of the title." This raises the key question of this chapter: Are Christians saints or sinners? The answer is found in how the Scriptures use the terms "saint" and "sanctified."

Saints

Paul frequently addresses his readers as "saints" (Rom. 1:7; Eph. 1:1; Col. 1:2). The Greek word for "saint" is *hagios*, which means to be "separated unto God." "Saint" thus refers not to the believer's character but rather to his or her state of being. This new state of being is based not on our achievements but rather upon God's act of setting us apart from the world and the dominion of sin for Himself. Jerry Bridges writes, "We are made saints by the immediate supernatural action of the Holy Spirit alone who works this change deep within our inner being so that we do, in fact, become new creations in Christ."[11]

In Acts 26:18, Paul describes this change of state as turning "from darkness to light and from the power of Satan to God, that they may receive forgiveness of sins and a place among those who are sanctified by faith in me." In Colossians 1:13, Paul states, "He has delivered us from the domain of darkness and transferred us to the kingdom [i.e., God's rule and blessing] of his beloved Son." In 2 Corinthians 5:17, Paul writes, "If anyone is in Christ, he is a new creation. The old has passed away; behold, the new has come." Thus, every believer, in this sense, is a saint.

Sanctified

In 1 Corinthians 1:2, Paul uses both terms. He begins, "To the church of God that is in Corinth, to those *sanctified* in Christ Jesus, called to be *saints*..."

Sanctification is most often thought of as a process, or ongoing work of God's free grace, within believers whereby they are being progressively and inwardly renewed and conformed into Christlikeness (moral renewal or growth in holy living, which is the fruit of sanctification). This is certainly true. However, the Scriptures use the term "sanctified" in a broader way. They distinguish between what theologians call *definitive* and *progressive* sanctification. In 1 Corinthians 1:2 and 6:11, Paul uses "sanctified" to speak of definitive sanctification. What then is definitive sanctification?

Let's start with some basics. The term "sanctified," much like "saint," means to be set apart, to separate. Horton writes, "God's sanctification separates people, places, and things away from their ordinary association for His own use."[12] For example, the utensils in the tabernacle and later the temple were said to be holy—meaning they were set apart for sacred purposes and were therefore distinguished from their common or ordinary use (Ex. 40:9–10).

The priests—and even their garments (Ex. 28:4)—were said to be holy unto the Lord because they were set apart for a divine purpose (Ex. 28:26). Animals used in sacrifice were called holy because they were set apart for a divine purpose (Lev. 23:19–20). The nation of Israel was set apart from other nations and declared to be holy unto the Lord.

> "I am the LORD your God, who has separated you from the peoples. You shall therefore separate the clean beast from the unclean, and the unclean bird from the clean. You shall not make yourselves detestable by beast or by bird or by anything with which the ground crawls, which I have set apart for you to hold unclean. You shall be holy to me, for I the LORD am holy and have separated you from the peoples, that you should be mine." (Lev. 20:24–26)

The New Testament carries over this same meaning and shows that sanctification is first of all God's act of setting us apart from the world for Himself.[13] Our definitive sanctification (i.e., God's act of setting us apart) finds its originating source in our election in Christ.[14]

In Ephesians 1:4, Paul writes, "even as He chose us in Him before the foundation of the world, that we should be holy [*hagious,* i.e., morally pure] . . ." In Colossians 3:12, Paul writes, "Put on then, as God's chosen ones, holy [*hagioi,* i.e., saints] and beloved . . ."

In his farewell address to the Ephesian elders, Paul said, "I commend you to God and to the word of his grace, which is able to build you up and to give you the inheritance among all those who are sanctified" (i.e., set apart by God; Acts 20:32). Hebrews 10:10 states, "by that will we have been sanctified [set apart by God] through the offering of the body of Jesus Christ once for all."

From these passages we see that every Christian is a saint—a separated one—because he or she has been sanctified—set apart—by God for God's own use.

We must not think, however, that because our state of being has changed that we are now sinless or perfect. Our unique experiences of failure and flaws, our crippling habits, endless addictions, and constant frustration about our inability to do the good that we long to do all clearly testify that we are like the apostle Paul who cries out, "Wretched man that I am! Who will set me free from the body of this death?" (Rom. 7:24; see vv. 14–24). Who can honestly claim to have perfectly fulfilled the Great Commandment, i.e., love for God and neighbor?

For example, no believer can claim to have perfectly conformed to all that God requires and forbids in the seventh commandment: "You shall not commit adultery" (Ex. 20:14). In Galatians 6:3, Paul says those who think they have perfectly kept God's law are deceived. Question 62 of the Heidelberg Catechism states, *"Even our best works in this life are all imperfect and defiled with sin"* (emphasis mine). Again, Question 114 asks, "But can those converted to God keep these commandments perfectly?" Here is the answer: "No. In this life even the holiest have only a small beginning of this obedience. Nevertheless, with earnest purpose they do begin to live not only according to some but to all the commandments of God."[15] In my church, we have a weekly corporate confession of sin. Having heard God speak to us in His law, we kneel in humility and confess together:

> Almighty God, Father of our Lord Jesus Christ,
> maker and judge of us all:
> We acknowledge and lament our many sins and offenses,
> which we have grievously committed by thought, word,
>   and deed
> against your divine majesty,
> provoking most justly your righteous anger against us.
> We are deeply sorry for these our transgressions;
> the burden of them is more than we can bear.
> Have mercy upon us,

have mercy upon us, most merciful Father;

for your Son our Lord Jesus Christ's sake,

forgive us all that is past;

and grant that we may evermore serve and please you

 in newness of life,

to the honor and glory of your Name;

through Jesus Christ our Lord. Amen.[16]

In other words, all who have been truly set apart by God do not disregard any part of God's law. All whom God has set apart for Himself sincerely seek to live in conformity to all that God forbids and requires in His law. But in this life saints will struggle and sin (see 1 John 1:5–2:2). This raises an obvious question: If we are saints and have been sanctified, why do we struggle? Why do we continue to sin?

The answer is that even though we are *already* set apart from the world by God for God, we are *not yet* glorified. The remnants of sin and the Adamic flesh still cling to us. This "already but not yet" reality is the source of the great tension and struggle we face.[17] We rightly become frustrated when our experience doesn't match our identity in Christ. Paul discusses this struggle in Galatians 5:17 and in greater detail in Romans 7. Martin Luther and the Reformers referred to this inner tension and struggle of the Christian by the Latin phrase *simul iustus et peccator*: *simul* (at the same time) *iustus* (just) *et* (and) *peccator* (sinner).

By this phrase, Luther and the Reformers didn't mean that a Christian who is still a sinner is an unchanged person. As we have just seen, by God's gracious actions we are made new creatures in Christ, indwelt by the Holy Spirit and set apart by God for Himself. Nonetheless, the Christian is still unjust in himself (i.e., he is partially sinful and partially righteous in terms of the slow process of sanctification).[18]

In Romans 6, Paul rejoices over the fact that he is justified, definitively set apart from the dominion of sin and alive in Christ. But, in Romans 7, he agonizes over the incongruity between the gospel fact of

Romans 6 and his ongoing battle with indwelling sin that keeps him from obeying God's law perfectly. This struggle with remaining sin need not discourage us. Why? In Romans 8, the struggling Christian of Romans 7 is not condemned (see Rom. 8:1)! The struggling Christian is alive in the Spirit and awaiting in the certainty and hope of his or her resurrection of the body and the renewal of creation.[19] But the Christian's desires will always exceed his or her experience in this life.

In Galatians 5:17, Paul argues that this conflict is not just the experience of immature Christians (sometimes called "carnal" Christians) versus those who are truly sanctified, "victorious" Christians. Rather, every believer experiences this constant, daily conflict between the flesh and the Spirit. This conflict is the normal Christian life in this present age.[20] In fact, it is the "already"—God's act of setting us apart and making us saints and giving us the gift of the Spirit—that creates an internal groaning for the consummation of the "not yet" (freedom from our struggle with sin, resurrection, and the renewal of creation; see Rom. 8:23).

REFLECTION

In answer then to the question, "Are Christians saints or sinners?" the reply is: *Every believer is a saint because every believer has been set apart by God, but at the same time he or she struggles with indwelling sin.*

Every believer is simultaneously justified and sinful (*simul iustus et peccator*). This reality causes our frustration and grief as we see the darkness of our own hearts. Therefore, the last thing we need is to be told is to try harder. We have *all* tried harder, but sin remains! Moral advice only deepens our despair. Even though we have been sanctified (set apart by God for God), our sinful desires do not simply disappear. We still live in the aftermath of original sin, which affects us every moment.

Therefore, Paul doesn't exhort the Corinthians to try harder or be better. He doesn't offer "relevant and practical" steps for overcoming sin in our life, which only impose more expectations and demands as conditions for success. He doesn't issue a call to enter the "higher" or "victorious" life for spiritual Christians. Nor does he offer an under-realized eschatology that says the world is irredeemable and that change is impossible or not worth pursuing. This would downplay the believer's new state of being as a saint and likely result in a passive approach to the Christian life. Instead, Paul calls believers to *action* (1 Cor. 6:9, 18, 20). As J. I. Packer writes, "The Christian's motto should not be 'Let go and let God' but 'Trust God and get going!'"[21]

In contrast to these unscriptural approaches, Paul reintroduces the Corinthians to a fresh knowledge of the gospel and its implications for sexual purity. Precisely because they are sanctified, Paul calls on the immoral Corinthians (and us!) to be holy. The gospel way of holiness is, "You *are* holy (i.e., definitive sanctification; set apart from the world by God for God); therefore *be* holy (i.e., obey what God requires in His moral law, which is the fruit of progressive sanctification by the indwelling gracious work of the Holy Spirit)."[22] Michael Horton writes, "The power of God is not only at work in Christ *for us* but is also 'the power at work *within us*' (Ephesians 3:20), so that, despite our own weakness, Christ's energies are at work within us by His Spirit (2 Corinthians 12:9–10)"[23] (emphasis added).

Paul understood that before the Corinthians could pursue holiness and growth in grace, they had to know that God had first set them apart from the world for Himself. The exhortation

> **We don't become saints by our actions. Rather, we are called to become more and more who we already are in Christ because of God's gracious actions toward us!**

then to "Be who you are" is infinitely different from moral pep talks or exhortations to try harder. Horton explains,

> In spite of the fact that the Corinthian church had become filled with immorality, strife, division, and immaturity, Paul begins both letters to this body by addressing them as "saints" (holy ones) and reintroduces the wonder of the gospel. Precisely because their status was defined by the gospel's indicatives, the apostle could recall them to repentance as the only legitimate response. Where most people think that the goal of religion is to get people to become something that they are not, the Scriptures call believers to become more and more what they already are in Christ. Because they were definitively sanctified or set apart as holy to the Lord, the Corinthians must reestablish proper relationships, order, and behavior in the church. Their practice must be brought in line with their identity.[24]

This is what you and I need to know. This is what Kate needed to know. We must be reintroduced constantly to the wonder of the gospel so that our practice can be brought into line with our identity. We need constant reminders of our new status before God—sainthood—and exhortations to live in light of this gospel reality. We are not called to try harder, to be something we are not. We don't become saints by our actions. Rather, we are called to become more and more who we already are in Christ because of God's gracious actions toward us!

We need to remember that we are already saints, separated unto God. But we must never forget that while we are *already* saints, saved from both sin's guilt and power, we are *not yet* saved from sin's presence. Therefore, we will continue to wrestle with our indwelling sin— we are *simul iustus et peccator*. We need to know that every believer is washed, sanctified, and justified, and yet, at the same time, struggles with indwelling sin.

50

Thus, we need to be continually reintroduced to the gospel! To pursue holiness, we need to know that Christ has saved us from the guilt and condemnation of our sin so we don't lose heart in our struggle. The glorious truth of the gospel is that even though we struggle—and often fail—we are not struggling from a position of judgment and condemnation! Why? The legal obstacles that might withdraw our new status as "saints" have been forever resolved![25] Because of Christ ("Thanks be to God through Jesus Christ our Lord!" Rom. 7:25), Paul, as the "wretched man" in Romans 7:24, confesses in faith, "There is therefore now no condemnation for those who are in Christ Jesus" (Rom. 8:1).

We needn't lose hope for real change because Christ has saved us from our corruption and slavery to sin. Because the dominion of sin has been overthrown, we are no longer slaves, helplessly unable to obey God. The gospel frees from guilt and empowers obedience (see Titus 2:11–14)!

Because of these gospel truths, even though we struggle, we don't have to lose hope. We needn't yield to despair. We don't have to throw up our hands in frustration and exhaustion. Yes, we know all too well the reality of the struggle. But the certain hope of resurrection and the renewal of all creation comforts us! We will struggle. But the good news is that we will ultimately prevail because the gospel always has the final word in our struggle: "Those who belong to Christ Jesus have crucified the flesh with its passions and desires" (Gal. 5:24). This is Paul's gospel strategy and logic. This is the gospel way of holiness. This is what "Do you not know?" means. And this is what Paul is going to teach us.

Chapter 3

WHO CAN'T INHERIT THE KINGDOM?

"I STARTED STRUGGLING with sexual immorality via pornography when I was fourteen," Derek confided. "I was raised in a Christian home and don't remember a time when I wasn't seeking Christ, but I couldn't shake my addiction to pornography. Because of my love for Jesus, the ongoing struggle was frustrating and disheartening. I tried it all. I read books on sexual sin, I did purity challenges with my Christian friends, and I made multiple commitments. I tried for years to 'beat my body into submission,' to no avail."

"On the contrary," he added, "I went backward. I was so beaten down, I honestly felt like walking away at many points and throwing in the towel on trying to live as a Christian."

As disheartening as my friend's losing battle with lust was, at least he was *fighting*. The Corinthian church didn't even try. It was, as we've repeated, a theological and moral mess. Members were unjustly suing fellow believers (1 Cor. 6:1–11) in pagan courts and arrogantly tolerating gross sexual immorality (1 Cor. 5:1–13; 6:12–20). In fact, Paul says they were tolerating a man guilty of engaging in incest with his stepmother—a kind of sexual immorality rejected even among pagans.

Then Paul addresses the problem of men in the Corinthian church who were arguing for their right to visit prostitutes.[1]

Admittedly, it is hard to imagine how such egregious behavior could have occurred in the Corinthian church. But the Corinthians, we must remember, had not come into the church as moral blank slates. Their ingrained habits and the surrounding culture's debauchery exercised a crushing downward pull on their sexual ethics. The wickedness and vice of Corinth are well documented.

The city was situated in a strategic shipping location on a four-mile-wide isthmus between the Ionian and Aegean Seas.[2] Corinth was a sex-obsessed seaport.[3] Gordon Fee notes that sexual sin was undoubtedly there in abundance, which is what one would expect in any seaport where money flowed freely, and women and men were available.[4]

The rampant sexual permissiveness of Corinth had clearly infected the Corinthian church. Whether the issue was suing one another in secular courts or tolerating sexual immorality in the church, members of this church displayed an arrogant preoccupation with self—self-indulgence, self-gratification, self-will—rather than faith in the gospel and submission to the ethics of God's kingdom. Fee observes, "In a culture where one could matter-of-factly say, 'Mistresses we keep for the sake of pleasure, concubines for the daily care of the body, but wives to bear us legitimate children,' the Judeo-Christian moral restrictions on human sexuality were not easily absorbed by pagan converts."[5]

That's why Paul, in 1 Corinthians 6:9–20, asks the Corinthians—and us—four questions. Each begins with the phrase, "Do you not know. . . ?" and is based on the gospel philosophy, "Be who you are." Paul's four questions are intended to take us back to the gospel and its life-changing implications. Please refer often to that critical passage of Scripture as you reflect on this book's arguments.

Paul rebukes the Corinthians by asking them whether they even grasp the basic facts of the kingdom of God.[6] Paul first asks:

"Do you not know that the unrighteous will not inherit the kingdom of God?" (vv. 9–11).

In verses 9–10, Paul warns, "Or do you not know that the unrighteous will not inherit the kingdom of God? Do not be deceived: neither the sexually immoral, nor idolaters, nor adulterers, nor men who practice homosexuality, nor thieves, nor the greedy, nor drunkards, nor revilers, nor swindlers will inherit the kingdom of God." Here the apostle is reminding the Corinthians of one of the first principles of the kingdom of God: that all who indulge in unrighteousness will not inherit it. Christianity is not only a system of doctrine and a form of worship but also a rule of life.[7] In a stinging tone, Paul asks the Corinthians, "Are you Christians and yet ignore the first and basic principle of the kingdom of God, of which you profess to be members?"

The kingdom of God is the binding theme of the Bible and was a dominant theme in Jesus' teaching (Matt. 4:23; Mark 1:15). The kingdom of God also played an important role in Paul's thinking and teaching. He makes five references to it in 1 Corinthians (1 Cor. 4:20; 6:9–10; 15:24, 50). As with Jesus, the kingdom of God was part of Paul's gospel. In Acts 28:30–31, Luke provides a summary of Paul's teaching in Rome, writing, "He lived there two whole years at his own expense, and welcomed all who came to him, proclaiming the kingdom of God and teaching about the Lord Jesus Christ with all boldness and without hindrance."

The importance of the kingdom of God in Scripture and in Paul's teaching raises some vital questions: What is the kingdom of God? How does it relate to the gospel? Who are the people excluded from the kingdom of God? Who are the people who inherit the kingdom of God? What does the kingdom of God have to do with one's daily life of sexual purity?

WHAT IS THE KINGDOM OF GOD?

The kingdom of God can be defined as "God's people in God's place under God's rule and blessing."[8] To live under God's rule is to live under His blessing.[9] The kingdom of God is first seen in the garden of Eden. Adam and Eve lived in God's place, the garden, in willing obedience to God's Word and rule and therefore enjoyed His covenantal blessings. However, when they disobeyed and rebelled against God, they forsook God's blessings and came under His covenant curses.

The devastating consequences for their disobedience were cosmic in scope. Not only Adam and Eve but also all mankind and all of creation were corrupted. But God, in a surprising act of grace, promises to restore His kingdom once again (see Gen. 3:15). God, as the great promise-keeping King, restores a people to be the willing subjects of His perfect rule. Each successive stage of this redemption, marked by a covenant, builds on the former until the fulfillment of His initial promise comes through Christ's first coming. The consummation of His promise will happen at Christ's second coming.

> **The kingdom of God then is both "already" and "not yet."**

The kingdom of God then is both "already" (1 Cor. 4:20) and "not yet" (1 Cor. 6:9–10; 15:24, 50). And so, we see that the Bible is an unfolding story about how God, the King, is faithful to His initial promise to restore His kingdom. This promise finds fulfillment and consummation through the person and work of Jesus Christ.

How does the kingdom of God relate to the gospel?

Currently, we live in what Vaughan Roberts calls "the proclaimed kingdom."[10] During our days as followers of Christ, God's kingdom spreads throughout the earth as the Holy Spirit works through the proclamation of the gospel (1 Cor. 6:11). Graeme Goldsworthy writes, "This is how the kingdom of God comes: Jesus exercises his kingly power through the scepter of his preached gospel."[11] Through the gospel of the kingdom, the Holy Spirit is gathering a people to be the willing citizens of God's rule and blessing. Through the gospel, God's people are brought into God's place—the church, which Paul calls the temple of God—to live under Christ's rule and blessing.

In 1 Corinthians 3:16, Paul describes the church as God's temple, the dwelling place of God. In chapter 6, verse 19, Paul says that the believer's own body is a temple of the Holy Spirit, i.e., the dwelling place of God.

This brings us to a third question concerning the kingdom of God.

What does the kingdom of God have to do with our daily life of sexual purity?

Paul's application of the kingdom of God to sexual purity is obvious: *because we are already citizens of God's kingdom, we are expected and enabled to live in a new way that is characterized by righteousness rather than unrighteousness.*

Simply put, "The law sends us to the gospel for our justification; the gospel sends us to the law to frame our way of life."[12] We receive the gospel freely. It empowers us to live in obedience to God's law, which expresses the standard of righteousness in God's kingdom. As God's people in God's place, we are now once again under God's rule and blessing. We have been set free from the condemnation and power of sin.

Therefore, we are not victims of uncontrollable passions and desires. We have been blessed with every spiritual blessing in Christ (Eph. 1:3), granted the gift of the Holy Spirit (Acts 2:38), and enabled to enjoy all the blessings of the new covenant (Jer. 31:31–33). Prior observes, "Citizens of such a kingdom were called to live in a special way: more than that, they were able to live in a distinctive way, and it was therefore doubly crucial for them to be different."[13]

Since these are gospel realities, Christians are not to be marked by arrogance, pride, self-will, and unrighteousness. We are not to live in opposition to God's law—the ethical standards of God's kingdom. Paul believed and taught that the kingdom of God had already been ushered into this present age (1 Cor. 4:20). It has been inaugurated by Christ's resurrection but not yet fully consummated (1 Cor. 6:9–10; 15:24, 50). Paul is saying: Because you have already been made a citizen of God's kingdom, act like it. Live like a citizen of God's kingdom. Be who you are. Just as you should stop suing one another (1 Cor. 6:1–10), you must also stop living in sexual immorality (1 Cor. 5:1–13; 6:11–20).

However, because the Corinthians had failed to grasp the basic facts of the kingdom of God, Paul issues a strong warning.

WHO IS EXCLUDED FROM THE KINGDOM OF GOD?

In 1 Corinthians 6:9–10, the apostle gives an illustrative rather than exhaustive list of the people who will *not* inherit the kingdom. Each of the sins in Paul's vice list violates God's moral law and illustrates a behavior of those outside the kingdom of God, who live in open violation of God's law. These sins characterize the fallen culture of Corinth in which the Corinthian church was living and from which the Corinthian church had been saved.

Paul's list warns us that certain behaviors cannot be a part of faithful Christian living and do not reflect the ethical standards of the kingdom.[14] Paul's vice list nearly parallels his list in 1 Corinthians 5:10–11, with the addition of adulterers, men who practice homosexuality, and thieves.

"Sexually immoral"—Heading the list are the "sexually immoral" (*pornoi*). This is a violation of the seventh commandment. This vice is most likely at the head of the list because it is the problem Paul is addressing in this context. "Sexually immoral" refers to any form of sexual behavior outside a monogamous, lifelong, heterosexual marriage (i.e., premarital, extramarital, and unnatural sex). The sexual ethic in God's kingdom is clear: abstinent singleness or heterosexual marriage. **"Idolaters"**—After "sexually immoral," Paul lists idolatry. "Idolaters" (*eidōlolatrēs*) refers to all who place their trust in anyone or anything other than the one true God who has revealed Himself in His Word and the Word, Jesus Christ.[15] Idolatry is a violation of the first and second commandments. Idolatry follows sexually immoral because both vices reflect the problem in 1 Corinthians.[16] Sexual immorality and idolatry go together. David Garland observes,

> His warnings about idolatry include warnings about sexual immorality (10:8). Paul shares the sentiment expressed in the Testament of the Twelve Patriarchs that "fornication is the mother of all wicked deeds; it separates from God and leads men to Beliar." . . . It is "the pitfall of life, separating man from God and leading to idolatry." . . . Fornication and idolatry go together (1 Cor. 5:10–11; 6:9; 10:7–8) because they belong to the same evil domain that warps what can be known about God, disfigures life, and wreaks havoc in society. Anyone who finds sex with a prostitute permissible is also likely to have no qualms about idolatry.[17]

Idolatry and sexual immorality were closely conjoined in Jewish thought.[18] Infidelity to one's spouse became a metaphor for infidelity to God. The Old Testament prophets frequently depicted God's relationship to Israel as that of a husband and wife (see Isa. 62:5; Jer. 3:14). Thus, Hosea represented Israel's sins—especially idolatry—as adultery (Hos. 4:1–19). Certainly, sexual immorality is one of the more visible idols of our sex-obsessed culture in America.

"Adulterers"—After idolatry, Paul lists "adulterers" (*moichos*). Adulterers refer to married persons who violate their vows and engage in sexual behavior outside of their marriage. Adultery is a violation of the seventh commandment.

"Homosexuality"—Following heterosexual sin, Paul now lists homosexual sin, "men who practice homosexuality." Like adultery, this too is a violation of the seventh commandment. The translation in the English Standard Version, "men who practice homosexuality," is actually composed of two different Greek words. The reason the ESV translates these two words in one descriptive phrase is for ease of public discourse on this subject.[19] However, in expositing Paul's meaning, we need greater precision.

First, Paul uses the word *malakos*, which literally means "the soft ones" and can be translated "effeminate males who play the sexual role of females."[20] With this term, Paul is referring to the passive partner in homosexual intercourse.[21] Second, Paul uses the word *arsenokoitēs*, which literally means "male-bedders" and can be translated "males who take other males to bed."[22] With this term, Paul is referring to the active partners in homosexual sexual intercourse.

We should pause here and acknowledge that many readers will recognize the challenges faced by those who take a biblical stance on matters of sexuality. Our current culture has obviously been undergoing significant transformation to its traditional mores, and Christians have had to respond, both corporately as the church and as individuals navigating issues with friends and family. Some local churches and denominations have even split over the issue of practicing same-sex relationships. My own denomination, the Anglican Church in North America, has issued a compassionate and comprehensive statement I commend to you.[23] Let's continue with Paul's list.

"Theft"—Following sexual sins, Paul also lists "thieves" (*kleptai*), referring to robbery. Theft is a violation of the eighth commandment.

"Greedy" (*pleonektai*) comes next and speaks of the state of desiring to have more than one's due; covetousness. Greed also violates the eighth commandment and goes hand in hand with thievery. Greedy, covetous people desire what belongs to others, and thieves act on their covetous, selfish desires. David Garland notes that greed applies to both rich and poor alike.[24] Moreover, greed is selfishness and a demand for more and more. Thus, greed can apply not just to money but also to sexuality, a selfish desire that is never satisfied, as David Garland observes: "The greedy are those who treat others only as objects for their gratification. Greed is related to insatiability and can express itself in multiple ways. The greedy include those who believe that their sexuality is a right, not a responsibility, and that they can express it in any way they choose with anybody they choose."[25]

"Drunkards" (*methysoi*) is self-evident. Excessive and uncontrolled drinking or drunkenness has no place among those who are citizens of God's kingdom. Paul joins drunkenness with unrestrained license or profligacy in Ephesians 5:18. Drunkenness could be placed under the seventh commandment. Drunkards throw off every restraint of modesty and shame. Astonishingly, drunkenness by way of selfish indulgence and indifference to others characterized the Corinthians' abuse of the Lord's Supper (see 1 Cor. 11:21). No wonder Paul issued such sobering warnings of God's judgment against those who abuse the Lord's Supper (1 Cor. 11:27–32).

"Revilers" (*loidoroi*) are verbally abusive people. This sin is a violation of the ninth commandment. Revilers abuse others with their speech (e.g., backbiters, slanderers, gossips, twisters of words, condemners, liars, etc.). Sinful speech betrays the sin of one's heart, as Jesus said, "out of the abundance of the heart the mouth speaks" (Matt. 12:34). God does not consider the sins of the tongue lightly. They are just as serious as unjust lawsuits, incest, and other forms of sexual misconduct and warrant the same punishment: exclusion from the kingdom of God.

"Swindlers" (*harpages*) take advantage of others to promote their own financial gain by extortion, false advertising, deceit, and so on. Swindling violates the eighth commandment.

These sins define and illustrate the unrighteousness that excludes human beings from the kingdom of God. However, I want to emphasize that Paul's list is not directed to Christians who struggle with the flesh (see Gal. 5:17). He is not referring to momentary lapses and failures. There is no condemnation for born-again believers who sin (Rom. 8:1). Paul recognizes that because Christians are at the same time saint and sinner (*simul iustus et peccator*), they will struggle and fail (Rom. 7).

Because the kingdom of God is "already but not yet," believers are not entirely free from sin in this life (Rom. 7:21–24; Gal. 5:17; 1 John 1:5–2:2). Summarizing the teaching of Scripture, the Canons of Dort, 5:1, states, "Those whom God, according to His purpose, calls to the communion of His Son, our Lord Jesus Christ, and regenerates by the Holy Spirit, He also delivers from the dominion and slavery of sin, though in this life He does not deliver them altogether from the body of sin and from the infirmities of the flesh."[26] Similarly, Article 9 in the Thirty-Nine Articles notes that this infection of nature remains even in those who are regenerate.[27]

Paul's warning applies to those who live in continual, open rebellion against God and have no inward delight to follow God's moral law. All who live in unrighteousness as a settled way of life will not inherit the kingdom of God. Paul repeatedly warned that perpetual, unrepentant immorality excludes the unrighteous from the kingdom of God (Gal. 5:19–21; Eph. 5:3–6; 1 Thess. 4:2–8). It demonstrates that a person is not a citizen of God's kingdom.

All the sins listed here by Paul share a common characteristic: self-indulgence, self-gratification, and self-will, rather than faith in Christ by means of the gospel and submission to the ethics of God's kingdom.

REFLECTION

As we reflect upon Paul's warning, let us remember three things.
1. Judgment is certain.
Judgment (exclusion from the kingdom of God) is the fate of the serially unrighteous. Paul's warning is no trivial matter. The seriousness

and urgency of Paul's tone ought to make a deep impression upon us. Some in the visible church "will not inherit the kingdom of God." Paul is warning us, "Do not be deceived. Let all who wish to live unrighteous lives be warned. To reject Christ's rule (kingship) and to live in open rebellion against His kingdom is disastrous!" Rather than inheriting God's kingdom, the unrighteous will be judged and excluded (see 1 Cor. 6:2).

2. We must guard against the tendency to be deceived.

Paul desperately wants the Corinthians to stop deceiving themselves. We see the danger of remaining under the spell of deception in Paul's imperative, "Do not be deceived!" Paul warns, "Do not be deceived. If you really think that gospel liberty is to be equated with lawless license, think again! Righteousness is the fundamental characteristic of God's kingdom. Those who practice unrighteousness as a settled way of life will not inherit the kingdom of God."

Paul is seeking to awaken us from the intrinsic deceitfulness of sin. Hebrews 3:13 says, "But exhort one another every day, as long as it is called 'today,' that none of you may be hardened by the deceitfulness of sin." In Ephesians 4:22, Paul exhorts believers to "put off your old self, which belongs to your former manner of life and is corrupt through deceitful desires."

> Sin presents itself to us as pleasing, good, and desirable. Thus, we can be easily deceived into thinking that we can indulge in sin without consequences.

The exceeding deceptiveness of sin makes temptation a lot more difficult. Sin presents itself to us as pleasing, good, and desirable. Thus, we can be easily deceived into thinking that we can indulge in

sin without consequences. But John Owen exposed this deadly mis-
conception, saying, "Herein lies no small share of the deceitfulness of
sin, by which it prevails to the hardening of men, and so to their ruin,
Heb. 3:13,—it is modest, as it were, in its first motions and proposals,
but having once got footing in the heart by them, it constantly makes
good its ground, and presseth on to some farther degrees in the same
kind."[28] Therefore, when we are tempted to yield to our illicit sexual
desires, we must heed Paul's warning: embrace Christ and His purifying gospel truths, and quickly turn away when tempted.

**3. Righteousness and unrighteousness will not coexist in the consum-
mation of God's kingdom.**

Nothing unrighteous, nothing impure, and nothing unholy or
corrupt will inherit the kingdom of God. In Revelation 21 and 22,
John sees a vision of how all redemptive history will end. We must
not overlook his warning that the unrighteous will *not* be in the New
Jerusalem. In Revelation 21:27, John warns that "nothing unclean will
ever enter it." Nothing. In Revelation 22:15, John warns that all who
succumb to the pressure and temptation of the surrounding pagan culture will be excluded, saying, "Outside are the dogs and sorcerers and
the sexually immoral and murderers and idolaters, and everyone who
loves and practices falsehood."

Why this total exclusion? Prior writes,

> The unrighteous cannot inherit the kingdom of God because
> God is altogether righteous. The unrighteous actually exclude
> themselves from the kingdom of a righteous God. They ex-
> clude themselves by their own chosen behaviour. Because
> God's kingdom reflects his own character or righteousness
> and compassion, those who insist on living by different stan-
> dards will not be there.[29]

This then is the first and basic fact of the kingdom of God: the unrighteous cannot inherit it. Any who persistently indulge in unrighteousness will not be there. Since unrighteousness cannot inherit God's kingdom in the future, we must not tolerate it now. Geoffrey B. Wilson states, "The ethics of the kingdom yet to come determine the morals of the kingdom that now is."[30]

However, as we will see, Paul's warning is not the final word on the matter. In an amazing and swift change, the apostle concludes his first argument by reaffirming the Corinthians' new status as citizens (saints) in God's kingdom. Paul says that some of you were once greedy, litigious idolaters and some of you were once sexually immoral idolaters. But now, in Christ by the Holy Spirit you are a new creation, a citizen of God's kingdom. Therefore, be who you are!

My friend Derek, whom we met at the beginning of this chapter, is beginning to live out his identity in Christ. Derek says that God's love has provided more power in his fight against sexual sin than his many self-centered attempts at self-discipline ever could.

"To be truly free from sexual sin one must experience a heart reformation," Derek says. "One must see that he is completely justified and beloved in the sight of God despite his heart problem. Ironically, this starts softening the heart to a pursuit of holiness."

Chapter 4

WHO CAN INHERIT THE KINGDOM?

STEVE IS A CHRISTIAN who had been taught a model of discipleship that basically said, "Your salvation is in jeopardy every time you sin. Get to work or God will drop you." So when he began to give in to sexual sin, he knew he was in big trouble.

"It didn't take long for that kind of teaching to crush me. I soon lost my assurance of salvation," Steve said. "I did my best to practice self-denial, and I even gained some outward conformity to the law. But all my striving did absolutely nothing to deal with the lust in my heart, neither could it restore to me any sense of peace. In fact, it made things worse."

In the last chapter, we encountered a chilling warning: the serially unrighteous will not be present in the consummation of God's kingdom. The matter is so gravely certain that Paul says it twice, providing an illustrative list of serial, unrepentant sins, a sign that one isn't truly in Christ, and thus that lead to exclusion from the kingdom of God. By directing the Corinthians forward to the consummation of God's kingdom, Paul wants to drive home the point: since unrighteousness cannot inherit God's kingdom in the future, it must not be tolerated in the present. The ethics of the kingdom yet to come determine the morals of the kingdom that already is.

In 1 Corinthians 6:9–10, Paul seeks to humble the arrogant, self-willed Corinthians by reminding them of their former lost condition in a state of unrighteousness. This is the pedagogical function of the law, to give us knowledge of our sin and misery to lead us to acknowledge the grace of God in Christ. As Calvin says, "For the greater the misery is acknowledged to be, from which we have escaped through the Lord's kindness, so much the more does the magnitude of his grace shine forth."[1]

In verse 11, the magnitude of God's grace shines forth brilliantly. "And such were some of you. But you were washed, you were sanctified, you were justified in the name of the Lord Jesus Christ and by the Spirit of our God."

This grace naturally leads us to two final questions regarding the kingdom of God. If the unrighteous cannot inherit the kingdom of God—and all are unrighteous—*who* can inherit the kingdom of God, and *how*?

The amazingly good news is that Paul's warning from the law in verses 9–10 is not the final word. In verse 11, the apostle reaffirms the Corinthians' remarkable transformation and new status as citizens (saints) in God's kingdom.

In verses 9–11, Paul contrasts their ugly past with their beautiful present ("You once were . . . but now you are"). Formerly, Paul says some of the Corinthians—not all—prior to their conversion were sexually immoral, idolaters, adulterers, homosexuals, thieves, greedy, drunkards, revilers, and swindlers—excluded from the kingdom of God. But now, having been granted life through Christ by the Holy Spirit, they are new creations, citizens of God's kingdom (note: the repeated "but" [*alla*] before each verb in the Greek of verse 11 adds emphasis to the Corinthians' break with their past).

There are hardly more hope-giving words in all of Scripture than 1 Corinthians 6:11, which is reminiscent of Paul's words in Ephesians 2:1–4: "But God..." Verse 11 is one of the most important theological statements in 1 Corinthians. In recounting the Corinthians' spiritual transformation, Paul provides three verbs.

Each verb illustrates how Christ exercises His kingly power through the scepter of His preached gospel and grants the unrighteous an inheritance in His kingdom.[2] These three verbs vividly set forth the Lord's kindness. Through them the magnitude of His grace shines forth.

There is great power and hope in these three verbs. Each directs our attention to the gracious action of the triune God with respect to our inheritance in the kingdom. Now let's focus on how Paul describes the Corinthians' spiritual transformation.

1. "But you were washed." (1 Corinthians 6:11b)

In describing their spiritual transformation, Paul answers the question, *How can the unrighteous come to inherit the kingdom of God?*

Through the preaching of the gospel, the Corinthians received regeneration as God's gift. God in His great wisdom has appointed the gospel to be the seed of regeneration and the food of the soul.[3] Regeneration is how a sinner enters (inherits) the kingdom of God and becomes a citizen of it. Jesus told Nicodemus that this supernatural rebirth is indispensable to seeing and entering God's kingdom (John 3:3, 5).

Regeneration highlights the fact that entrance into the kingdom is based solely on grace. Clearly the Corinthians possessed no merit. They were excluded from the kingdom of God. They were, as Paul says in Ephesians 2:1, *dead* in their trespasses and sins. How then can a spiritually dead and morally defiled person inherit the kingdom of God? God in His great grace reaches down to the lowest depths of human need and meets all the requirements necessary to make an unrighteous sinner a citizen of His kingdom.[4]

This radical change cannot be attributed to any human resources or merit. The word "inherit" helps us here. Paul uses the word "inherit" (*klēronomeō*) twice in verses 9–10 to show that God's kingdom is an inheritance bestowed upon a son through the privilege of adoption.[5] The kingdom of God is the inheritance of a son, not the wage of a worker.

There are two aspects by which regeneration is to be understood: re-creation and purification.[6] Both constitute the total change that occurs in a sinner's heart when the Holy Spirit raises him from death to life and delivers him from the domain of darkness and transfers him to the kingdom of God's beloved Son. In *re-creation*, the Holy Spirit, through the announcement of the gospel, sovereignly and graciously raises to life in Christ those who are spiritually dead.[7] In Ephesians 2:4–5, Paul writes, "But God, being rich in mercy, because of the great love with which he loved us, even when we were dead in our trespasses, made us alive together with Christ." In short, the Holy Spirit re-creates in newness of life, as Paul writes in 2 Corinthians 5:17, "If anyone is in Christ, he is a new creation. The old has passed away; behold, the new has come" (see 2 Cor. 4:6).

Regeneration also entails *purification*, whereby the Holy Spirit purges our inner defilement. I suspect Paul begins with this emphasis because he is addressing sexual immorality, which defiles both body and spirit. Because nothing unrighteous or unclean will enter God's kingdom (1 Cor. 6:9–10; Rev. 21:27), the unrighteous must be spiritually cleansed to enter the kingdom.

The "you were washed" wording stresses the removal of dirt and refers to the inward, spiritual cleansing of the filth of past sins.[8] In describing the Corinthians' regeneration, Paul says they were washed; spiritually cleansed from the filth of their former sins listed in verses 9–10. In regeneration, the Holy Spirit graciously purges the defilement of our hearts, which would otherwise exclude us from His kingdom.

This was Jesus' point when He told Nicodemus, "Unless one is born of water and the Spirit, he cannot enter the kingdom of God."[9] The Old Testament parallel connecting "water" and "spirit" comes from Ezekiel 36:25–26, where Ezekiel prophesies, "I will sprinkle clean water on you, and you shall be clean from all your uncleannesses, and from all your idols I will cleanse you. And I will give you a new heart, and a new spirit I will put within you. And I will remove the heart of stone from your flesh and give you a heart of flesh." Some see in Paul's words an allusion to baptism. Certainly baptism serves as a sign and seal of regeneration, though it does not effect it. If Paul does have baptism in mind, it is to teach believers how to properly use their baptism in the daily pursuit of sanctification. Baptism is a powerful, visible sign and seal (guarantee) that flashes like a neon sign: "All your filth and shame has been washed away!"[10]

Assurance of being washed and made clean is particularly vital for those who are guilty of sexual sin. Sin leaves a person defiled and full of shame as a result of being unclean and naked before God, who is perfectly holy.[11] Shame and remorse over sin is brought about by conviction of the Holy Spirit and leads to repentance. When Adam and Eve fell, they immediately became aware of their "nakedness" before God and attempted to hide (see Gen. 2:25 and 3:7–11). Nothing is more frightening than to be fully exposed before a holy God in an unclean state.

This shame before a holy God is the proper response of those guilty of sexual sin, whereas for those who have been victims of sexual crimes, there is a different kind of shame experienced. Ed Welch writes, "Shame from being sexually victimized is the best known example of victimization shame. Women who have been sexually violated can feel overwhelmed by what they perceive as the gaze of God and others." The one who is sinned against, especially in this manner, needs counsel.[12] In this context, shame warps a person's understanding of their true identity in Christ. Shame and a sense of defilement are natural tendencies and obscure their understanding of their relationship before God, but the reality is, in Christ, they are *already* washed and made clean, without cause for shame.

Though not the total answer, the doctrine of regeneration—particularly the purification aspect—along with baptism is critical in helping people overcome the crippling effects of shame. The good news—as signified and sealed in baptism—is that all who are re-created by the Spirit are also cleansed by the Spirit. Through baptism, God wants to teach us that the blood and Spirit of Christ wash away sins just as water washes away dirt from our bodies. But more importantly, He wants to assure us by this divine pledge and sign that the washing away of our sins spiritually is as real as physical washing with water.[13] Thus, one's baptism is a powerful weapon in pursuing holiness and defeating shame. Calling to mind and reflecting upon one's baptism is a needful but much neglected duty, which is to be performed by us all our lives, especially in the time of temptation.

> God, by His grace, washes us, cleansing us from all manner of defilement, giving us a pure and undefiled new nature.

Paul's point: since the Corinthians have been washed, they must not defile themselves with sexual sins. Sexual sin leaves us defiled. God, by His grace, washes us, cleansing us from all manner of defilement, giving us a pure and undefiled new nature. In regeneration, the Holy Spirit purges our defilement, makes us clean, and re-creates us so that we can obey and pursue holiness and purity. Going back to Ezekiel 36, in verse 27, God, after cleansing the sinner and putting a new heart in him, says, "I will put my Spirit within you, and cause you to walk in my statutes and be careful to obey my rules."

Regeneration then is the basis of all change in heart and life. In regeneration, God not only cleanses us from our defilement from sin (washing us and making us clean), He also addresses our slavery to sin (re-creation/giving us a new heart). By giving us new hearts, the Holy Spirit changes our desire for evil into a desire for good. Regeneration is the root of all true obedience to God and His law. It is our basis for pursuing holiness and purity.

Second, in describing their conversion, Paul deals with the doctrine of definitive sanctification.

2. "But you were sanctified." (1 Corinthians 6:11c)

Through the preaching of the gospel, the Corinthians received the gift of sanctification. As we learned in chapter 2, Paul isn't talking about the process of sanctification, which is commonly referred to as *progressive* sanctification (i.e., the work of God's free grace, whereby we are renewed in the whole man after the image of God, and are enabled more and more to die unto sin, and live unto righteousness).[14] Rather, he is speaking of *definitive* sanctification (to be set apart). By God's gracious action (election, Eph.1:4), the Corinthians had been set apart from their former sinful state (vv. 9–10) and made saints. This is how Paul begins his letter: "To the church of God that is in Corinth, to those sanctified in Christ Jesus, called to be saints. . . ." (1 Cor. 1:2).

In directing the Corinthians to their definitive sanctification, Paul is saying, "Because you were sanctified (set apart), you must not pollute yourselves again."

If regeneration is the basis of all change in heart and life, definitive sanctification is its purpose. God has claimed the Corinthians for His own and conferred upon them the status of saints. God had set them apart for Himself. He made them holy, suitable citizens for His kingdom. They were set apart to pursue holiness, which stands in stark contrast to their former sinful lifestyles.

Paul is saying, "Because you have been set apart for holy rather than unholy purposes, repent of your arrogant toleration of sexual immorality and pursue holiness as is fitting for saints."

Sexual sin leaves us polluted, set apart for unholy purposes. So what does God do in His kingdom? He sanctifies us. He sets us apart for holy purposes. Precisely because the Corinthians are sanctified (definitive sanctification; set apart from the world for God), they (and we!) are called to be holy (progressive sanctification; to fulfill the purpose for which they had been set apart; to live in the sphere of God's holiness, 1 Thess. 4:3–8).[15] As I noted previously, religion calls on people to become something they are not. Christianity, however, calls on Christians to be who they already are in Christ.

This brings us to the third aspect of Paul's description of the Corinthians' gracious transformation.

3. "But you were justified." (1 Corinthians 6:11d)

Through gospel preaching, the Corinthians received the gift of justification. How can the unrighteous come to inherit the kingdom of God? The unrighteous Corinthians (vv. 9–10) were *declared* righteous by the King!

Justification is the chief article of Christian doctrine and life. Martin Luther said, "This doctrine is the head and the cornerstone. It alone begets, nourishes, builds, preserves and defends the church of God; and without it the church of God cannot exist for one hour."[16]

What then is justification? Justification is God the judge's declaration that the unrighteous is righteous even while being inherently unrighteous. God justifies the ungodly (Rom. 4:5). God's verdict is true (not a legal fiction) and just (not unjust) because it is rendered on the basis of Christ's perfect righteousness alone, which is imputed to sinners by grace through faith alone. Consequently, all whom God justifies are counted by God *just as if they have never sinned* and *just as if they have always obeyed*. Though they were "unrighteous," God justifies the Corinthians so that they can be counted "righteous" and inherit the kingdom from which they were formerly excluded.

Why does Paul remind the Corinthians of their justification? Sexual sin results in paralyzing guilt, regret, and self-condemnation. But since the Corinthians have been justified, they must not condemn themselves. The doctrine of justification frees the believer from self-condemnation and paralyzing guilt and regret because it provides a perfect foundation of righteousness.

Because of the "already but not yet" aspect of the kingdom, all believers are simultaneously justified and sinful (we are not perfect yet!). Though sin's dominion has been overthrown, sin still indwells us. Therefore, we experience a continual struggle, a tension that Paul describes in Galatians 5:17: "For the desires of the flesh are against the Spirit, and the desires of the Spirit are against the flesh, for these are opposed to each other, to keep you from doing the things you want to do."

Because of this continual struggle—even though we are delivered from the dominion and guilt of sin—we

> **Because of the "already but not yet" aspect of the kingdom, all believers are simultaneously justified and sinful.**

continually fall short of the perfect righteousness God requires in His law. Since our faith is weak and imperfect, it cannot serve as the true ground of our justification. If it did, we would have an imperfect, uncertain, and shaky ground for confidence before God.

Sexual sin, particularly, leaves us paralyzed under crippling guilt. How easy it is to forget that we enjoy a right standing with God. *Mark this: the struggling believer is right with God, but the serially unrepentant "professing believer" is excluded from the kingdom of God.*

Because of our struggle with indwelling sin, we often forget the justifying grace of God in Christ. So Paul reminds the Corinthians (and us!), "Do you not know that you have been justified?"

The truth of justification keeps us persevering in the midst of our continual struggle with sin. It keeps us grounded in our confidence before a holy God. So if regeneration is the basis of all change in heart and life and if definitive sanctification is the purpose for this change, justification is the motivation to continue pursuing a life of holiness. God's declaration of our justification keeps us from becoming paralyzed with an accusing conscience. As already mentioned in chapter 1, the Heidelberg Catechism Question 60 beautifully captures this truth (emphasis mine):

Q. How are you righteous before God?

A. Only by true faith in Jesus Christ; that is, *although my conscience accuses me that I have grievously sinned against all the commandments of God, have never kept any of them, and that I am still prone always to all evil,* yet God, without any merit of mine, of mere grace, grants and imputes to me the perfect satisfaction, righteousness and holiness of Christ, as if I had never committed nor had any sins, and had myself accomplished all the obedience which Christ has fulfilled for me, if only I accept such benefit with a believing heart.[17]

Every day we sin. And every day our conscience condemns us on this basis. Therefore, we must by faith bring the verdict of our conscience—guilty!—into line with the verdict of God's declaration—justified! The gospel announces that all who are in Christ are no longer condemned: "There is therefore now no condemnation for those who are in Christ Jesus" (Rom. 8:1). And so, we must continually remind ourselves and our burdened consciences that our sin is forgiven and that God has reckoned to us the perfect righteousness of Jesus. Until we believe the gospel truth that we are dead to sin's guilt and no longer condemned, we will not persevere in the pursuit of holiness. Moreover, we will not trust Christ for the strength to subdue sin's power.[18]

Only a self-conscious awareness of justification will allow us to persevere in holiness. A kindergarten-level understanding of justification will not suffice. We must meditate on our justification often and pray over it until we receive the Holy Spirit's assurance in our head and heart. But we cannot overlook an indispensable truth: justification is not a license to justify immoral behavior. If it were, Paul would hardly use it in a context where he is exhorting believers to a faithful pursuit of purity! Union with Christ is the fountain of all true obedience to God. Question 64 of the Heidelberg Catechism asks, "Does this teaching not make people careless and wicked?" Here's the answer: "No. It is impossible that those grafted into Christ by true faith should not bring forth fruits of thankfulness."

Justification and sanctification are the double benefits received upon one's union with Christ.[19] Thus, justification and sanctification *never* appear separately. John Calvin, commenting on 1 Corinthians 1:30, writes (emphasis mine),

> From this, also, we infer, that we cannot be justified freely through faith alone without at the same time living holily. *For these fruits of grace are connected together, as it were, by an indissoluble tie, so that he who attempts to sever them does in a manner tear Christ in pieces.* Let therefore the man who seeks to be justified through Christ, by God's unmerited goodness, consider that this cannot be attained without his taking him at the same time for *sanctification*, or, in other words, being renewed to innocence and purity of life.[20]

Similarly, in his *Institutes*, Calvin writes, "*Christ justifies no one whom he does not at the same time sanctify.* These benefits are joined together by an everlasting and indissoluble bond, so that those whom he illumines by his wisdom, he redeems; those whom he redeems, he justifies; those whom he justifies, he sanctifies."[21]

The faith that receives justification also receives sanctification. These double benefits are to be distinguished but never separated. We counter the false notion that one desires to be delivered from the punishment of sin but does not desire to be delivered from the slavery of sin by saying that no one can trust Christ for true salvation without trusting Him for holiness.[22] Such an understanding of faith is actually a terrible presumption.[23] Walter Marshall, an English pastor, said,

> True gospel faith makes you come to Christ with a great thirst, that you might "drink of living water"—by which Christ means His sanctifying Spirit (John 7:37–38). True gospel faith makes you cry out earnestly for God to save you—not only from hell but from sin as well. "Create in me a clean heart, Oh God, and renew a right spirit within me" (Psalm 51:10). When you seek salvation by faith in Christ, holiness is a major part of the salvation that Christ freely gives you. You cannot divide salvation. You cannot have the forgiveness of Christ without the holiness of Christ.[24]

Faith produces good works. Yet good works are the *fruit* of justifying faith, not its cause. Article 12 in the Thirty-Nine Articles states:

> Albeit that Good Works, which are the fruits of Faith, and follow after Justification, cannot put away our sins, and endure the severity of God's Judgment; yet are they pleasing and acceptable to God in Christ, and do spring out necessarily of a true and lively Faith; insomuch that by them a lively Faith may be as evidently known as a tree discerned by the fruit.[25]

No one is justified because he is sanctified. Good works are always the fruits of a true and lively faith, never its cause. As the influential English pastor and theologian William Perkins noted, justification by works is a mere fiction.[26]

So then, in order to pursue holiness, we must learn to live in a continual state of conscious justification.[27] We have to be assured of the truth of the gospel, which says that in God's eyes we are as righteous today as we will be in the consummation of His kingdom.

If we are going to live a sexually pure life, we must have assurance of our justification. We must receive the comfort of the gospel. Though this sounds counterintuitive and perhaps even permissive, it isn't! This is the gospel way of holiness. Marshall writes, "If you are going to live a holy life, you first have to receive the comfort of the gospel. If you are going to receive the comfort of the gospel, you have to be completely assured that you indeed have a personal relationship with Christ. . . . Having assurance of these things is absolutely necessary if you are going to keep the law of God and live a holy life."[28]

Again, Marshall notes,

> Faith purifies your heart, and enables you to live and walk in holiness, as Christ lives in you. Your faith will never do this for you unless you have some assurance of your relationship with Christ. . . . You cannot use the grace of God to enable you to live a holy life if you are not sure you have truly received the grace of God. You cannot live a holy life if you do not believe that you are dead to sin and alive to God through Christ. You cannot live a holy life if you do not believe that you are not under law but under grace. You cannot live a holy life if you do not believe that you are a member of Christ, the temple of his Spirit, and his dear child.[29]

The gospel assures us that our right standing before God can never change because we have been given the imputed righteousness of Christ. So in your daily struggles and failures with indwelling sin, remember: God justifies us! He frees us from all condemnation. He reckons to us a perfect foundation for righteousness (Christ's righteousness). A self-conscious awareness of justification is the basis for persevering in holiness. It frees us from self-condemnation and empowers us for the first time in our lives to pursue a life of obedience.

Paul establishes all of these gospel truths—regeneration, adoption, definitive sanctification, justification—in the doctrine of the Trinity. He gives to us a "God-centered Gospel."[30] Paul writes that God has effected salvation "in the name of the Lord Jesus Christ and by the Spirit of our God" (v. 11). Everything that God does comes from the Father in the Son through the Spirit.[31]

Here, Paul emphasizes that the saving work of Christ is the *procuring (purchase) cause* of our salvation.[32] Regeneration, adoption, definitive sanctification, and justification come to us through His life, death, and resurrection. However, as long as Christ remains outside of us, He is of no benefit to us. Christ must not only be given *for* us; He must also be given *to* us.[33] Therefore, the internal work of the Holy Spirit is the *effectual cause* of our salvation.

In the gospel Christ accomplished the work of salvation *for us*, and, through the announcement of Christ in the gospel, the Holy Spirit applies the work of Christ *in us*. Christ is the source of all blessings to us; and the Holy Spirit communicates Christ and all of His blessings to us. In verse 11, Paul has in view the total spiritual transformation made possible through Christ's work *for us* and effected by the Holy Spirit's work *in us*, all of which originate from the sovereign, loving plan of God the Father.

REFLECTION

As we reflect on Paul's teaching regarding the spiritual transformation of the Corinthians (and us), let us remember:

1. Paul's words are filled with hope for sinners.

Paul says that God, through the good news, cleansed the Corinthians from their former defilement, adopted them as sons, set them apart for His holy purposes, and declared them righteous in His sight.

In short, He made them citizens of the kingdom of God. The good news of the kingdom is that He can do the same for *you* today, if only you accept this gift with a believing heart.

2. All who are transformed by the gospel are expected to live out the implications of the gospel. The gospel brings about a whole new sexual ethic in God's kingdom. All three of the saving actions by God that Paul mentions demonstrate the purpose for which God graciously reconciles us to Himself by the free forgiveness of our sins. The gospel is intended to drive us to pursue purity, to persevere in true holiness, and to forsake and despise our former state of unrighteousness.

Regeneration is the *basis* of all change. Definitive sanctification is the *purpose* for all change. And justification and adoption together are the *motivation* in the pursuit of change. J. I. Packer writes,

> That justification frees one forever from the need to keep the law, or try to, as the means of earning life, it is equally true that adoption lays on one the abiding obligation to keep the law, as the means of pleasing one's newfound Father. Law-keeping is the family likeness of God's children; Jesus fulfilled all righteousness, and God calls us to do likewise. Adoption puts law-keeping on a new footing: as children of God, we acknowledge the law's authority as a rule for our lives, because we know that this is what our Father wants. If we sin, we confess our fault and ask our Father's forgiveness on the basis of the family relationship, as Jesus taught us to do—"Father ... forgive us our sins" (Lk 11:2, 4). The sins of God's children do not destroy their justification or nullify their adoption, but they mar the children's fellowship with their Father. "Be holy, for I am holy" is our Father's word to us, and it is no part of justifying faith to lose sight of the fact that God, the King, wants his royal children to live lives worthy of their paternity and position.[34]

Paul is reminding the Corinthians (and us!) that we are to live differently than the world precisely because God in Christ and by the Holy Spirit has cleansed us from the defilement of our past sins, set us apart from our former sins to belong to Him, and has already forgiven us and given us a right standing with Himself and adopted us as His royal children.

Simply put, Paul is exhorting us on the basis of the gospel to become what we already are in Christ. Here is his appeal in contemporary language:

> You were once unrighteous, but now, by the grace of God, you are righteous. You were once excluded from the kingdom of God. But now you are citizens of God's kingdom. However, you don't understand who you are. You don't know that you are an inheritor of the kingdom of God. You don't know that you are a people of the Spirit. Instead, you are arrogantly tolerating sexual immorality among you as if you are still excluded from God's kingdom. But you are now a citizen of God's kingdom. You are a new creation. You are a saint in God's kingdom. Therefore, stop unjustly suing one another in pagan courts and stop tolerating gross sexual immorality. These vices characterized your prior life. But this is no longer who you are. Therefore, live like a citizen of God's kingdom, since this is who you now are.

Paul then reminds us of our spiritual transformation in order to deter us from reverting to our former miserable state. He is exhorting us to change by reminding us that we inherit the kingdom of God because of the gracious work of Christ and the Holy Spirit (v. 11).

3. The gospel is not a license to indulge in the sins of unrighteousness.

Clearly the gospel of the kingdom doesn't lead to moral laxity or a laissez-faire attitude toward sin. The gospel does not lead to arrogant toleration of unrighteousness. God is not in the business of white-washing sins but of transforming sinners.[35] The gospel brings about a transformation of individuals, issuing in a new sexual ethic. The previous vice list warns that the serially unrighteous will not inherit the kingdom. But, Paul says, that is what some of us were. Now, in Christ, we are different.

The gospel grants regeneration. As a result, all who are new creations in Christ possess a Spirit-induced desire to follow and live by the ethics of God's kingdom. The citizens of this kingdom do not dismiss the King's laws. Rather, they take them seriously and by faith obey them, living out the implications of the gospel.

4. The gospel is the ministry of the Holy Spirit.
We must not lose sight of Paul's emphasis upon the transforming work of the Holy Spirit. The coming of the Holy Spirit into the world signifies the coming of God's kingdom—the presence of the future. The presence of the Holy Spirit signifies that the realities of the consummated kingdom are already at work. The Holy Spirit is now bringing the power and ethics of the new creation—the consummated kingdom—into this present evil age (Titus 3:5-6).

The Holy Spirit is the author of faith. He creates faith in our hearts (John 3:5; Eph. 2:8) by the preaching of the gospel (Rom. 10:17; 1 Peter 1:23-25).[36] The Holy Spirit is the agent of regeneration, sanctification, and justification. The Holy Spirit is the Spirit of adoption (Rom. 8:14-17). Yet how often do we ignore the indispensable role of the Holy Spirit because of the excesses of others? Gordon Fee writes, "The Spirit belongs to the creed and to our theology but is all too often left there, so that the Spirit's genuinely transforming and empowering work is often left until the Eschaton, rather than experienced in the process of arriving there."[37]

Apart from the working of the Spirit, the gospel would fall upon deaf ears. Therefore, we must pray for and expect by faith the transforming and empowering work of the Holy Spirit in our midst. We must not forget that the gospel is the ministry of the Holy Spirit (2 Cor. 3:8) and that we are the people of the Spirit. He is the one who alone brings about the spiritual transformation of the unrighteous into citizens of the kingdom through the announcement of the gospel.

Steve, whom we met at the start of this chapter, now understands this indispensable truth. "I have learned and am continuing to learn that yes, the gospel is enough," Steve says. "The same gospel that I first believed when I came to faith in Christ is the same gospel that I stand in and the same gospel that I use to fight against my sin and the lies of the enemy." In using that gospel to overcome his sin, Steve is demonstrating that he is among those who will indeed inherit the kingdom of God.

Part 2

*What Is
the Body?*

1 CORINTHIANS 6:12–20A

Chapter 5

OUR BODIES WILL LIVE FOREVER

"I BECAME A CHRISTIAN in the early 1990s," Arthur told me, "and I had a struggle with pornography ever since I could remember. It was in our house growing up, as well as in our grandparents' house. There had never been a conviction in my heart about it until I was made alive by Christ." The ready availability of porn sparked a downward spiral in Arthur's heart, mind, and body. He continued,

> It was and is a heart-wrenching sin struggle. You give in, and you repent, and the same cycle repeats itself. It destroys you as a person. This kind of besetting sin keeps you from God's Word because you feel like a hypocrite just reading it. The thing about this sin is that it is an addiction that encompasses our mind and body and reprograms our brains as though we need another dose like heroin.

Such is the power of sexual sin. Yet it need not have the last word. While it can take a devastating toll in this world, a proper focus on the next world can drain sexual sin of its seemingly urgent power.

As we begin the second section of this book—What Is the Body?—let's briefly recap Paul's argument so far. In 1 Corinthians 6:9–20, the apostle asks the Corinthians four questions, each beginning with "Do you not know . . . ?"

Paul's questions rebuke the Corinthians' attempted justifications for their sexual immorality. Their glib slogans,[1] which we will examine starting now, revealed that they didn't know the gospel and its implications for their sex lives. Therefore, Paul seeks to reintroduce the Corinthians to the gospel, which alone has the power to motivate them to flee immorality (v. 18a) and lead them to glorify God in their bodies (v. 20b).

First, in verses 9–10, Paul warns that the serially unrighteous will not be present in the consummation of God's kingdom.

> Or do you not know that the unrighteous will not inherit the kingdom of God? Do not be deceived: neither the sexually immoral, nor idolaters, nor adulterers, nor men who practice homosexuality, nor thieves, nor the greedy, nor drunkards, nor revilers, nor swindlers will inherit the kingdom of God.

But Paul's warning from the law is not the final word. In an amazing and swift change, in verse 11 he reaffirms the Corinthians' conversion and new status as citizens (saints) in God's kingdom.

> And such were some of you. But you were washed, you were sanctified, you were justified in the name of the Lord Jesus Christ and by the Spirit of our God.

By directing their attention to the future consummation, Paul is driving home this point: *Since unrighteousness cannot inherit God's kingdom in the future, it must not be tolerated in the present.* The ethics of the kingdom yet to come determine the morals of the kingdom that already is.

And by reaffirming their status as citizens of God's kingdom, Paul exhorts the Corinthians (and us!) to live differently precisely because God in Christ by the Holy Spirit has: (1) re-created them in newness of life and cleansed them from the defilement of their past sins (washed/regenerated); (2) set them apart from their former sins to belong to Him (sanctified/definitive sanctification/election); (3) forgiven them and given them a right standing with Himself (justified); and (4) granted them an inheritance (adoption as sons!).

On the basis of these gospel blessings, Paul is exhorting the Corinthians simply to become who they are. Next, he proceeds from the affirmation of verse 11 to an attack on the Corinthians' theological justification for sexual immorality. Paul writes,

"All things are lawful for me," but not all things are helpful. "All things are lawful for me," but I will not be dominated by anything. "Food is meant for the stomach and the stomach for food"—and God will destroy both one and the other. The body is not meant for sexual immorality, but for the Lord, and the Lord for the body. And God raised the Lord and will also raise us up by His power. (1 Cor. 6:12–14)

Two words dominate Paul's arguments in verses 12–20: "sexual immorality" and "body"[2]:

"All things are lawful for me," but not all things are helpful. "All things are lawful for me," but I will not be dominated by anything. "Food is meant for the stomach and the stomach for food"—and God will destroy both one and the other. The *body* is not meant for *sexual immorality*, but for the Lord, and the Lord for the *body*. And God raised the Lord and will also raise us up by his power. Do you not know that your *bodies* are members of Christ? Shall I then take the members of Christ and make them members of a prostitute? Never! Or do you not know that he who is joined to a prostitute becomes one *body* with her? For, as it is written, "The two will become one flesh." But he who is joined to the Lord becomes one spirit with him. Flee from *sexual immorality*. Every . . . sin a person commits is outside the *body*, but the *sexually immoral* person sins against his own *body*. Or do you not know that your *body* is a temple of the Holy Spirit within you, whom you have from God? You are not your own, for you were bought with a price. So glorify God in your *body*.

As we will come to see, due to a radically flawed understanding of Christian freedom, some of the Corinthians maintained they were free to do anything they wanted sexually. Paul, therefore, wants the Corinthians to reflect on a gospel-centered view of the body and freedom in order to flee sexual immorality (v. 18a) and to glorify God in their bodies (v. 20b).

First Corinthians 6:12–20 is one of the New Testament's paramount theological passages about the body's importance. Paul argues that our bodies belong to Christ and thus we are not free to do anything we want with it. The resurrection validates the moral importance of the body and demonstrates that it has a glorious destiny that motivates the believer to flee sexual immorality and to glorify God in his or her body. While Paul issues the commands to flee sexual immorality and to glorify God, he grounds them in the truth of the gospel (the imperative always flows out of the indicative, never the reverse).

In contrast, the Corinthians, under the pretense of wisdom, arrogantly claimed that the body is temporary and unimportant, and the only thing that matters is the spiritual realm. They concluded that it made no difference what they did with their bodies. *Note carefully*: the fallen heart of mankind will always seek some way to justify immoral behavior.

We learn here that immoral living flows from theological error, as reflected in the slogans they were advocating and living by.[3] In response, Paul enters a dialogue with the Corinthians to confront and correct their false theology. In verses 12–13, Paul is countering the Corinthians' erroneous views about freedom and the human body.[4]

A FALSE VIEW OF FREEDOM (V. 12)

One of the favorite slogans of the Corinthians is, "All things are lawful for me" (Paul repeats it again in 1 Cor. 10:23). They used it to argue that "I am free to do anything."[5] Paul corrects their false view of Christian freedom by offering two counter slogans of his own.

First, in response to the slogan, "All things are lawful for me," Paul responds, "but not all things are *helpful*" (emphasis mine). In the context, Paul is referring to sexual sin. The word "helpful" is the Greek word *sympherō*, which means "to be advantageous, help, confer a benefit, be profitable/useful."[6] Paul's point is that self-indulgent sexual license doesn't contribute to my good or the good of the covenant community—the church. No sin is advantageous, helpful, profitable, or beneficial (see 1 Cor. 6:9–10).

For example, the Scriptures portray the destructiveness of King David's moral failures, which harmed his family for generations. Proverbs 6:26–31 warns that succumbing to sexual temptation leads to disaster—in fact, committing adultery is fatal. Proverbs 6:32–34 warns, "He who commits adultery lacks sense; he who does it destroys himself. He will get wounds and dishonor, and his disgrace will not be wiped away. For jealousy makes a man furious, and he will not spare when he takes revenge."

The promotion of sexual "freedom" within our culture has brought devastating physical, psychological, emotional, and spiritual consequences: broken marriages, divorce, shattered homes, diseases, and so on. Sexual sin leaves men and women crippled with shame and guilt. It makes us feel defiled and dirty. It leads to crushing guilt, an accusing conscience, and suffocating loads of regret. Like the church in Corinth, we live in a sex-obsessed society that suffers from incredibly devastating and destructive consequences.

To Paul, the real question is not whether an individual is free to do anything he or she chooses. Rather, the real question of Christian freedom is whether such behavior is helpful to oneself.[7] Paul repeats this slogan in chapter 10, verse 23 and joins it with the idea of "building up" (*oikodomein*) within the community.

Christian conduct that properly accords with the gospel is not based on so-called freedom of choice. Instead, it first asks, "Is my conduct spiritually beneficial to myself and to others? Does it build up or tear down spiritually?"

Let's remember that Paul was the apostle and champion of Christian freedom among the Gentiles. Some Bible teachers suggest that the Corinthians' radical view of Christian freedom may have come from a misunderstanding of Paul's teaching.[8] Paul did indeed teach that believers are free from the Mosaic law as a *covenant for life*—but this was never its purpose (see Gal. 3:17–21). Paul never taught that believers were free from the moral law of God as a *rule of life*. Paul always qualified the Christian's freedom as "in Christ." One is free to act, provided one's actions are grounded "in Christ" and guided by the moral law rather than by fleshly self-indulgence. Samuel Bolton writes, "Christ has freed us from the manner of our obedience but not from the matter of our obedience."[9]

Christian freedom is *never a license to indulge the sinful desires of the flesh*. As Paul reminded the Galatians, "you were called to freedom, brothers. Only do not use your freedom as an opportunity for the flesh, but through love serve one another" (Gal. 5:13).

Second, Paul states that Christian freedom must not become a means of *bondage*. The Corinthians asserted, "All things are lawful," but Paul replies, "I will not be dominated by anything." Christian freedom does not lead to enslavement to anything or anyone.

Again, the context is sexual sin. There is hardly a more enslaving sin than this. Sexual sin is all-consuming. It is like the Lay's potato chips slogan, "Betcha can't eat just one!" The more you indulge in sexual license, the more it controls your life.

As the champion of Christian freedom, Paul was free to live in the grace of Christ. However, he refused to misuse his freedom in a way that would enslave him to any sin. Either Christ and the transforming power of the gospel will dominate you, or the fallen passions and desires of your flesh will.

Paul would not allow himself to be mastered by anything but Christ! How thoroughly does this commitment influence your daily life? When we seek to live a self-consciously gospel-centered life, we will not *want* to be dominated by anything or anyone but Christ! This was the all-controlling reality of Paul's life.

Paul would not allow himself to be mastered by anything but Christ! How thoroughly does this commitment influence your daily life?

The Corinthians failed to understand how harmful and damaging unrestrained sexual license is to everyone involved. And they failed to understand how unrestrained sexual license gains control of and dominates those who indulge in it.

Next, Paul confronts and corrects the Corinthians' false view of the body.

A FALSE VIEW OF THE BODY (V. 13)

The second slogan the Corinthians used to justify their sexual license was, "Food is meant for the stomach and the stomach for food." The Corinthians reasoned, "Just as food is meant for the stomach and the stomach for food, so the body is meant for sexual activity and sexual activity for the body. Since God will one day destroy the body, it doesn't matter what we do with our bodies. Our behavior is of no moral consequence."

Greek dualism scorned the physical world and favored the "higher" knowledge and wisdom of "spiritual" existence.[10] Such an erroneous philosophy explains why the Corinthians possessed a defective view of the body. Because the Corinthians were influenced by their culture rather than the gospel, they reasoned that the acts of the body had no eternal significance or value. Paul responds by stating a basic fact of a gospel-centered life: "The body is not meant for sexual immorality, but for the Lord, and the Lord for the body" (v. 13b; note the comparison in verse 13, "food for stomach/stomach for food" versus "body for the Lord/the Lord for the body"). The believer's body belongs to the Lord.

Question 1 of the Heidelberg Catechism asks, "What is your only comfort in life and in death?" Here's the answer: "That I, with body and soul, both in life and in death, am not my own, but belong to my faithful Savior Jesus Christ."[11]

Having corrected the false views of Christian freedom and the body in verses 12–13, Paul will now set forth a gospel-centered view of the body in verse 14.

A CHRISTIAN VIEW OF THE BODY (V. 14)

In verse 14, Paul writes, "And God raised the Lord and will also raise us up by His power." This is a confirmation of the basic truth he asserts in verse 13. It is a Christian—gospel-centered—view of the body. Resurrection confirms that the believer's body belongs to the Lord and not to sexual immorality. Because the body belongs to the Lord, the ultimate end of the believer's body is not destruction (v. 13a) but resurrection (v. 14).

For Paul, the resurrection is of paramount importance. In 1 Corinthians 15, he gives the most extensive discussion of the resurrection in all of Scripture. The apostle argues that Christ's death for our sins, His burial, and resurrection are of first importance for the Christian's faith and life (1 Cor. 15:3). New Testament scholar Anthony Thiselton notes how Paul sets forth "an early creed which declares the absolute fundamentals of Christian faith and on which Christian identity (and the experience of salvation) is built."[12] Thus, all three saving acts of Christ are to have the foremost place in our confession and daily lives.

It is also important to note how Paul argues that Christ's resurrection is the central part of the gospel. As vitally important as Christ's death for our sins and burial are (and they are!), neither is good news without Christ's resurrection. Paul hangs everything on the claim to the historical, bodily resurrection of Jesus Christ (1 Cor. 15:12–19). Concerning the centrality of the resurrection, Graeme Goldsworthy writes,

> Evangelical thinking has tended to stress, rightly, the substitutionary atoning death of Jesus. Sometimes this is at the expense of the importance of the resurrection. . . . We should never take away from the importance of the death of Christ, but the centrality of the resurrection in the apostolic faith is just as important. . . . The resurrection was the Father's "Amen" to the finished work of Christ.[13]

Because the resurrection is paramount, it has important implications for the believer's daily life of sexual purity. The gospel teaches us that our bodies have a glorious destiny! Apparently, many Corinthian

Christians thought that salvation did not involve the body.[14] But Paul emphatically states that salvation involves the material and immaterial part of man—the whole person, not just the soul. Christ lived, died, was buried, and rose again to save not just our souls but also our bodies. In fact, our salvation involves the whole of physical creation itself (1 Cor. 15; Rom. 8:18–23).

Every citizen of God's kingdom now is moving toward the consummation of God's kingdom in the future (v. 14)! Our destiny is eternal life in a new heaven and a new earth—resurrection—where the righteous will dwell forever in a physical, bodily existence (Rev. 21:1–4). Richard Hays writes,

> The body belongs to the Lord Jesus, and God has confirmed his concern for the body by raising the Lord Jesus; this act of power declares God's ultimate promise to raise us also (cf. Rom. 8:11 and 1 Corinthians 15 in its entirety). . . . The body is not simply a husk to be cast off in the next life; the gospel of Jesus Christ proclaims that we are to be redeemed body, soul and spirit (cf. 1 Thess. 5:23–24; Rom. 8:23). Salvation can never be understood as escape from the physical world or as the flight of the soul to heaven. Rather, the resurrection of the body is an integral element of the Christian story. Those who live within that story, then, should understand that what they do with their bodies in the present time is a matter of urgent concern.[15]

Paul's emphasis on the resurrection should forever silence the implicit dualism that is so often passed off as Christian.[16] Consider, for example, choruses and slogans that talk about the world not being our home or how we're just "passing through." These phrases in common parlance show how an implicit Greek dualism has infected Christian thought. It places little to no value on the physical, created world that

God pronounced as "very good" (Gen. 1:31). The belief that the spirit is immortal, but the body (along with the rest of creation) is destined for destruction is pagan (1 Cor. 6:13a).[17]

Too many believers suspect that they are going to be in some kind of ethereal place and exist in some kind

> **"What will I be like when I die?" Our souls and bodies will be reunited and made like Christ's glorious body.**

of disembodied state when they die. In contrast, the Christian view confesses, "I believe in . . . the resurrection of the body" (Apostles' Creed).[18] The Heidelberg Catechism in Question 57 asks, "How does 'the resurrection of the body' comfort you?" Here's the answer: "Not only my soul will be taken immediately after this life to Christ its head, but even my very flesh, raised by the power of Christ, will be reunited with my soul and made like Christ's glorious body."[19]

To answer believers who wonder, due to the influence of pagan philosophy, "What will I be like when I die?" the answer, according to the gospel, is that at the resurrection we will be like Jesus (see Phil. 3:20–21). Our souls and bodies will be reunited and made like Christ's glorious body. This is the hope of the gospel!

Now, how does all of this apply to our life of sanctification and the daily battle against sexual immorality? How does this understanding of the resurrection help when you are sitting in front of your computer? My friend Rick illustrates the power of living in light of the resurrection in the battle against sexual temptation.

"My mindset was set in what I could gain from what I thought I was entitled to," he told me. "This worldview led me to eventually take hold of my sexuality as my own, indulging in pornography and eventually partaking in sex outside of marriage, completely defiling myself."

Rick felt he had rights to his own body in a way similar to those in the church in Corinth believed. Then he was regenerated by the Holy Spirit and became aware of his sexual immorality. After learning the implications of the resurrection, he repented.

"I see how offensive the attachment of that specific sin is to a body that is not mine," Rick said, "and that will one day be resurrected by His power."

So many believers have been influenced by an implicit Greek dualism that we don't long for resurrection or grow in purity. But when the resurrection becomes central in our thinking, this gospel truth purifies us and motivates us in our daily battle with all sexual temptation and sinful desires of the flesh. As 1 John 3:2–3 reminds us, "Beloved, we are God's children now, and what we will be has not yet appeared; but we know that when he appears we shall be like him, because we shall see him as he is. And everyone who thus hopes in him purifies himself as he is pure." Placing our hope in our future resurrection has a purifying effect now.

Such assurance that our bodies belong to the Lord and are destined for a glorious future with Him reminds us that our bodies do not belong to sexual immorality.

> **He will raise our bodies on the last day. The final resurrection validates the moral importance of what one does in his or her body now.**

Such continual, self-conscious gospel-centeredness has a powerful, purifying effect on our daily lives.

And we must not forget that, in a sense, the believer is already spiritually resurrected, which is signified and sealed in baptism. In Colossians 2:12, Paul writes that believers have already "been buried with him in baptism, in which you were also raised with him through faith in the powerful working of God, who raised him from the dead." Paul makes a similar argument in Romans 6:4: "We were buried therefore with him by baptism into death, in order that, just as Christ was raised from the dead by the glory of the Father, we too might walk in newness of life."

Once again, we see that Paul is simply arguing, "Be who you are." Because you have already been raised with Christ spiritually, His resurrection power is at work in your life. Believers have been raised to walk in newness of life (to live as citizens of God's kingdom rather than as outsiders who are excluded from God's kingdom; see 1 Cor. 6:9–11). We are *called* to walk in newness of life precisely because we *can*!

We must not think of the body and the physical world as things to be rejected, subdued, or indulged because they are of no significance for—or even a hindrance to—"real salvation," which has to do with the "soul." By raising Christ from the dead, God confirms the importance of the body and His physical creation, which He pronounced very good (Gen. 1:31). As we have seen, Paul devotes all of 1 Corinthians 15 to the doctrine of resurrection, including the certainty of bodily resurrection. Here, in 1 Corinthians 6, Paul appeals to this hope of bodily resurrection to confront the bodily sin of sexual immorality and motivate believers to glorify God with their bodies.

Rejecting the belief that the body is morally irrelevant and has no place in Christ's redemptive work in the present age or in the age to come, Paul emphatically asserts the resurrection of the believer's body. The bodily resurrection of the believer proves that the body is not meant for sexual immorality. Rather, the body is for the Lord, and the Lord is for the body. This is confirmed in the fact that He will raise our bodies on the last day. The final resurrection validates the moral importance of what one does in his or her body now. The application is obvious: set your hope fully on the resurrection and this will lead to purity.

Then Paul deals with one final question regarding the resurrection:

"How will it come about?" Look at his assuring words at the end of verse 14: "God raised the Lord and will also raise us up *by his power.*" The believer's resurrection will be effected by God's power. The resurrection is the greatest demonstration of God's power (Rom. 1:4; 2 Cor. 13:4; Phil. 3:10). Nowhere is our need for God's power more clear than in resurrection. Paul's reference to God's power emphasizes the fact that our resurrection results from the gracious power of God, not the natural ability of man.[20]

Note how Paul ties the believer's resurrection to Christ's (he will make the same argument in chapter 15, verse 23, "Christ the first fruits, after that those who are Christ's at his coming"). Just as the Father raised Christ from the dead, He will raise us also by His power. By virtue of our union with Christ, *His* destiny is also *our* destiny. Because Christ was raised, the believer's body is also destined to be raised by God's power. Paul writes in Philippians 3:21 that Christ "will transform our lowly body to be like his glorious body, by the power that enables him even to subject all things to himself."

The resurrection of the believer then is precisely what gives meaning, responsibility, and significance to our bodily existence now. Again, we see how Paul's eschatology plays a controlling factor in our daily life (see vv. 9–11, where Paul appeals to the consummation of the kingdom of God). As Gordon Fee writes, "The final consummation looks for a new heaven and a new earth; and in that new order the body is raised so that God's people will experience the final wholeness that God intended."[21]

Our friend Arthur, from the beginning of this chapter, has begun to experience in part the wholeness that one day, in the resurrection, will be fully his. "I am now pointed to what Christ has done for me," he says, "and now I can live in accord with that truth. It is not I, but Him, who lives in me. I am now seeing more and more victory as time goes on. The lust in my heart is still overwhelming at times, but the real growth to obey my Father out of gratitude has just begun."

REFLECTION

Your body is not your own. It belongs to the Lord because it is destined for resurrection. Therefore, you are not free to selfishly indulge in unrestrained sexual license. Your behavior has important moral significance and consequences. Christ is the Lord of your body and ruler of His kingdom. Because you are now a citizen of His kingdom, you have a new identity. You live according to a new sexual ethic and are bound for a new eternal destiny. Therefore, in light of this gospel truth, you are called to live according to this new standard of kingdom righteousness rather than the old worldly unrighteousness, which characterized your previous life when you were excluded from the kingdom of God (vv. 9–11).

The Corinthians had a faulty view of the body and Christian freedom because they didn't know the gospel and its implications. Once again, we see that the gospel is at stake. This is not simply about resolving an ethical question.[22] The gospel (specifically the resurrection) has direct ethical implications on how you are to conduct yourself. We believers need to continually rediscover and relearn the gospel and its implications for the Christian life. For the gospel is to serve as the plumb line for all our thinking, speaking, teaching, and living.[23]

Chapter 6

OUR BODIES ARE UNITED WITH CHRIST

IN THE FIRST CHAPTER, we met Trisha. She was unable to stop the sexual sin pouring out of her husband's life, which greatly affected her, and she was understandably in emotional agony. She felt defeated, and she was defeated. She needed a new perspective. Caring, mature Christian friends came alongside this couple with recommendations for sexual addiction therapy, teaching, counseling, and self-reflection. And Trisha is now gaining a new understanding of who she is in Jesus, as the therapy alone would have been helpful only to a point had it been separated from a gospel-centered paradigm. She says:

> I finally have gotten to a point where I can hear and receive the gospel. I can truly believe that I am worthy in Christ. I have my own voice because of what Christ has done for me. I have meaning, purpose, and am loved just the way that I am, because of Christ. It is by the sheer grace of God that I've learned to love myself and love my husband through all of the pain.

Christ is indeed the answer, as Trisha is learning. In the last chapter, we reflected on the glorious and life-changing truth that our bodies will live forever, because of Him. We saw how the coming resurrection validates the moral importance of the physical body today. Therefore, we Christians are not free to engage in unrestrained sexual license. As Calvin teaches, "It is a base thing to prostitute our body to earthly pollutions, while it is destined to be a partaker along with Christ of a blessed immortality and of the heavenly glory."[1] The resurrection empowers us to flee sexual immorality (1 Cor. 6:18a) and to glorify God in our bodies (v. 20b).

But there is more encouragement to gain by reflecting on the body from a Christian perspective. Having appealed to the doctrine of resurrection, Paul now appeals to the doctrine of union with Christ in order to demonstrate that our bodies belong to the Lord. The doctrine of union with Christ is of paramount importance. John Murray notes, "Nothing is more central or basic than union and communion with Christ. . . . Union with Christ is really the central truth of the whole doctrine of salvation not only in its application but also in its once-for-all accomplishment in the finished work of Christ."[2] Neglect of this central doctrine results in a gravely distorted view of the Christian life.[3]

In response to those Corinthians who sought to justify their sexually immoral behavior, Paul asks: *Do you not know that your bodies belong to Christ because they are in union with him?* (vv. 15–17). Paul writes,

Do you not know that your bodies are members of Christ? Shall I then take the members of Christ and unite them with a prostitute? Never! Do you not know that he who is joined to a prostitute becomes one body with her? For it is written, "The two will become one flesh." But he who is joined to the Lord becomes one spirit with him.

Before we dive into Paul's argument, let's look at the background and context of the problem he is addressing. Put simply, some of the Corinthian men were going to prostitutes and arguing for the right to do so.[4] Admittedly, Christian men arguing for the right to visit prostitutes seems rather extraordinary to many of us today. While this is not a justification, it is helpful to understand that prostitution was both legal and acceptable in ancient Mediterranean culture.[5] It was generally looked upon as a lawful act (see v. 12, "All things are lawful for me"). Richard Hays writes,

> Prostitution was not only legal; it was a widely accepted social convention. The sexual latitude allowed to men by Greek public opinion was virtually unrestricted. Sexual relations of males with both boys and harlots were generally tolerated. . . . Thus, the Corinthian men who frequented prostitutes were not asserting some unheard-of new freedom; they were merely insisting on their right to continue participating in a pleasurable activity that was entirely normal within their own culture.[6]

Calvin notes, "It is probable, that the Corinthians even up to that time retained much of their former licentiousness, and had still a savor of the morals of their city."[7] The ethical standards of Corinth rather than the gospel and its implications were the driving motivation behind the Corinthians' immoral behavior.

This fact raises an important issue. Sanctification for many believers is painfully slow and sometimes nearly imperceptible. It takes time for the gospel to peel back layer after layer of sin in our lives. Some of the Corinthian men were still being influenced by their fallen pagan culture rather than the gospel. We need to humbly remember that even though *we* do not have a problem with Christian men arguing for their right to visit prostitutes, the first-century culture of Corinth doesn't differ all that much from ours.

Men and women frequently indulge in sexual immorality in our culture through the internet, television, magazines, books, our smart devices, and so on. Sexual immorality may not be as grossly evident as it was in Corinth, but it is just as rampant in our culture—perhaps more so due to digital technology, which makes sexual immorality accessible with a simple double-click of a mouse.

Given these similarities, what can we learn from Paul's approach in order to combat this ever-present moral challenge?

> **The Holy Spirit creates faith in our hearts by the preaching of the gospel. Through this gift of faith, we are *legally* and *vitally* united to Christ in both soul and body.**

In verses 15–17, Paul responds to the Corinthians' attempt to justify—as illustrated by their slogans—their unrestrained sexual license, as seen in arguing for their right to visit prostitutes. The apostle does so by appealing to the doctrine of our union with Christ. This section amplifies his statement in verse 13 that the "body is for the Lord and the Lord for the body." He begins in verse 15 with a question that is really a rebuke: "Do you not know that your bodies are members of Christ?"

The believer's body is for the Lord (and the Lord for the believer's body) not only because, as we have seen, that God will raise it up by His power (vv. 12–14), but also because those bodies are "members" (*melos*) of Christ (v. 15). The word "members" is a term used to speak of the parts of the body. Through the gospel and faith, the Holy Spirit not only unites our souls to Christ, but also our physical bodies. As the Heidelberg Catechism begins, ". . . I am not my own, but belong body and soul, in life and in death, to my faithful Savior Jesus Christ."[8]

The Holy Spirit is the bond of our union with Christ. It is through the "secret energy of the Spirit, by which we come to enjoy Christ and all His benefits."[9] The Holy Spirit creates faith in our hearts by the preaching of the gospel. Through this gift of faith, we are *legally* and *vitally* united to Christ in both soul and body. Commenting on the believer's union with Christ, Jerry Bridges writes,

> Our legal union with Christ entitles us to all that Christ did for us as He acted in our place, as our substitute. Our vital union with Christ is the means by which He works in us by the Holy Spirit. The legal union refers to His objective work outside of us that is credited to us through faith. The vital union refers to His subjective work in us, which is also realized through faith as we rely on His Spirit to work in and through us.[10]

Though our union has two aspects—legal and vital—it is *one* union (two sides of the same coin). As we will see, 1 Corinthians 6:15–17 addresses our legal union with Christ and 6:18–20a speaks of our vital union (i.e., our bodies are temples of the indwelling presence of the Holy Spirit of Christ).

Before we proceed, keep in mind that the body is one of Paul's favorite metaphors to speak of the church (see 1 Cor. 10:17; 12). In 1 Corinthians 12:27, he writes, "Now you are the body of Christ and individually members of it." In Ephesians 4:15–16, Paul writes, "Rather, speaking the truth in love, we are to grow up in every way into him who is the head, into Christ, from whom the whole body, joined and held together by every joint with which it is equipped, when each part is working properly, makes the body grow so that it builds itself up in love."

The church is a living body, and the life of the church comes from Christ to whom she is united. Christ's power gives life and fruit to the church. Without Him, we can do absolutely nothing (John 15:5).

Paul's body metaphor in 1 Corinthians 12 is concerned with the relationship of the "members" to one another. Here in chapter 6, Paul's concern is with the believer's relationship to the Lord Himself.[11]

Paul's reasoning in verses 15–17 is very tightly connected to verses 12–14:

- The body of the believer belongs to the Lord because of resurrection (vv. 12–14).
- The body of the believer also belongs to the Lord by virtue of his or her legal union with Christ (vv. 15–17).
- Because the believer's physical body is "joined" to Christ's own "body," God the Father has set into motion the reality of the believer's resurrection.[12]
- Because we are legally united to Christ, we can say that when He died on the cross to suffer the penalty of sin, we died on the cross.
- When He was buried, we were buried.
- When He was raised, we were raised spiritually in the first resurrection and will be physically in the second resurrection (i.e., the consummation of God's kingdom; see 1 Cor. 15).

Thus, the believer can confidently say, "His resurrection is my resurrection. Christ's glorious destiny is my glorious destiny." Paul emphasizes this point in 1 Corinthians 15:22: "For as in Adam all die, so also in Christ shall all be made alive." All that Jesus is and did *we* are and did because of our legal union with Him.

Because our legal union is a reality, Paul asks the immoral Corinthians, "Shall I then take the members of Christ and make them members of a prostitute? Never!" (v. 15b). We are not our own but are joined *body and soul* to Christ. Paul's argument is quite explicit. He suggests an unthinkable reality. Paul is arguing that the Corinthian believers are so closely united with Christ that all who visit prostitutes are actually taking Christ's body and joining it to the body of a prostitute! Elsewhere in Scripture we see that whatever is done to the believer is also done to Christ. For example, in Acts 9:4–5 Jesus asks Paul (Saul) on the Damascus Road,

"Saul, Saul, why are you persecuting me?"
And he said, "Who are you, Lord?"
And he said, "I am Jesus, whom you are persecuting."

Who was Saul persecuting? Believers! In Galatians 1:13, Paul says, "For you have heard of my former life in Judaism, how I persecuted the church of God violently and tried to destroy it." His actions constituted a violent persecution of Christ Himself. Christ is so closely united to His people that whatever is done to them is done to Him.

But that is not the end of it. Paul is arguing in 1 Corinthians 6:15–17 that Christ and His people are so closely united that Christ is joined in their actions! When the believer participates in sexual immorality, he or she is taking Christ's members (body) and joining them to that which is impure, defiled, and unholy (i.e., in the context, taking Christ's body and joining Him to a prostitute's body). Such blasphemy is unthinkable!

Paul further expounds this thought in verses 16–17. He writes, "Or do you not know that he who is joined to a prostitute becomes one body with her? For, as it is written, 'The two will become one flesh.' But he who is joined to the Lord becomes one spirit with him."

For the second time in this brief passage, Paul asks the Corinthians, "Do you not know?" Sexual immorality—in this case, prostitution—cannot be regarded as "lawful" (v. 12) or simply the satisfying of a natural physical desire (v. 13). That's because unlawful sexual behavior creates an unholy, enduring bond between a man and a woman. David Garland explains,

Sexual union creates an enduring bond. The verb κολλάω (*kollaō*) implies that the man and the prostitute are wedded together even if there are no wedding vows. They may regard their union as only a temporary liaison—he to gain sexual release, she to gain a living—but it is more entangling than that; neither is free from the other when they part company.[13]

The physical union of a husband and wife is analogous but not equal to the legal and vital union between Christ and His people (Eph. 5:30–32). Christ's union with His people is far deeper.

Paul grounds his argument in Genesis 2:24, "The two will become one flesh." To be sure, Paul is not suggesting that union with a prostitute is equivalent to the union of a husband and wife. The union of a husband and wife in marriage is a holy union. The union of a man and woman outside of marriage is an unholy union. Yet sexual immorality still retains some faint, though marred, resemblance to marriage.

Paul is making the point that sexual immorality creates a real bond—albeit unholy—between a man and woman. The expression "the two become one flesh" is true and proper in terms of marriage alone. But Paul applies it to those who commit sexual immorality because there is a joining of two individuals in a polluted and impure bond.[14]

Hear carefully then the apostle's point: since a believer is united to Christ both soul and body, his or her immoral actions create an unholy bond between Jesus' body and his or her sin (in this case some of the Corinthian believers were joining Christ to prostitutes!).

Paul drives this point home in verse 17: "But he who is joined to the Lord becomes one in spirit with Him." The believer's union with Christ in verse 17 is described with the same verb used in verse 16 to characterize union with a prostitute (*pornē*). In fact, this same verb is used in the Septuagint in Genesis 2:24,[15] when Moses writes, "A man shall leave his father and his mother and hold fast to [cleave to (*proskollaō*)] his wife, and they shall become one flesh."[16]

In Jeremiah 13:11, the prophet says that the Lord caused the Is-raelites to cleave to Him: "For as the loincloth clings (*kollaō*) to the waist of a man, so I made the whole house of Israel and the whole house of Judah cling to me (*kollaō*), declares the LORD, that they might be for me a people, a name, a praise, and a glory, but they would not listen" (LXX).[17]

The essence of our response to the covenant of grace is to cling or belong to the Lord in order to be a people for His name and praise.[18] In Acts 15:14, James, at the Jerusalem Council, confirms Peter's argument that God was now including the Gentiles "to take from them a people for his name."

We are called to belong to Christ both in soul and in body. Since believers are in union with Christ, we cannot engage in unrestrained sexual license or immorality. Engaging our body in an illicit sexual union outside of marriage is to join Christ to this unholy union as well.

A basic and yet vital implication of the gospel is that our bodies—not just our souls—are *members of Christ*. Since the believer's body belongs to the Lord by resurrection and union, unrestrained sexual license is out of bounds. Rather, the Holy Spirit through the gospel empowers us to obey the seventh commandment[19]—"flee sexual immorality" (v. 18a) and "glorify God in your body" (v. 20b; see Ezek. 36:25–27).[20]

REFLECTION

Paul, in verses 15–17, shows that union with Christ is far more than an idea to be discussed in a systematic theology class. Paul is teaching us that union with Christ is our reference point for all our sexual behavior and the foundation of a sexually pure life. Our bodies do not belong to us. They belong to Christ in a manner analogous but not equal to the union of the bodies of a husband and wife.

When we commit sexual immorality, we are joining Christ's body to something sexually immoral, impure, and unholy. Our union with

Christ should highlight the utterly reprehensible nature of this sin. A self-conscious awareness of our union with Christ exercises a powerful, purifying effect on our daily lives.

In other words, a self-conscious awareness of our union with Christ leads us to obey the seventh commandment, both in what it forbids, "flee sexual immorality," and in what it requires, "glorify God in your body."

As well, this shows us how to teach abstinence to our children. Abstinence is only half of what the seventh commandment requires! It is not enough just to abstain!

If we teach only abstinence, and don't teach how abstinence is grounded in and motivated by the gospel, young people are going to be far less motivated to pursue sexual purity and may even react negatively. And if we teach only abstinence (fleeing sexual sin) but don't teach our children to live pure and disciplined lives, both within and outside of marriage, we will end up with moralistic idolaters in the place of sexual idolaters.

Moralism is the enemy of the gospel. As destructive and defiling as sexual sin is to the individual and the church, moralistic idolaters ultimately are far more destructive and Christ-denying. This is so because they substitute Christ and His righteousness for a Christ-denying *self*-righteous hypocrisy.[21] In so doing, they shift the ground of justification from Christ to self, erecting all manner of extrabiblical requirements for holiness!

So what does it look like to be self-consciously focused on our union with Christ when we are tempted with immorality? What happens every time we are tempted to look at pornography on our computer, to watch an immoral program on TV, to lust for a bikini-clad female at the beach or a skimpily dressed male in the gym, or by a sweet word from a coworker?

And what happens when we receive an email or a friend invitation from an old flame? How do we respond when we receive a charming smile at a neighborhood gathering? What do we do when loneliness fills our heart and passion comes knocking at the door?

Relying on our self-discipline or self-righteousness will lead to disaster. Self-focus cannot protect us from temptation. We need to look to Christ and our union with Him. We need to remember that when we break the seventh commandment, we are joining Christ to our unholy actions. Sexual sin is about much more than satisfying our private, unholy cravings. It is dragging the Holy One into our den of iniquity—simply unthinkable!

As Calvin says, "While God the Father has united us to His Son, what wickedness there would be in tearing away our body from that sacred connection, and giving it over to things unworthy of Christ."[22]

Are you beginning to see now how the gospel and its implications are so exceedingly purifying? Are you starting to see how living by faith and the gospel produces the fruit of holiness? What you *believe* (union with Christ) governs how you *live* (fleeing sexual immorality and pursuing purity and thus glorifying God). When the gospel and its implications rather than the fallen culture and the flesh dominate your life, it is inconceivable that you would ask Jesus to join you in unrestrained sexual license of any kind.

> **A self-conscious understanding of the gospel will govern how you think, what you say, and how you act. This truly is *good news!***

Would you take the sinless, radiant, risen Holy Son of God and join Him to the sinful, polluting filth of your sexual immorality? Are you going to take Christ's fingers and click on a porn site? Are you going to direct His eyes to lust after a man or woman? Are you going to take His ears and indulge in lewd conversations? Would you dare take the members of

Christ and make them members of your adulterous affair?

A conscious focus on your union with Christ will lead you to forcefully respond like Paul, "*mē genoito*," which means, "Never," "By no means," "God forbid!"

Joining Christ to sexual immorality is an utterly revolting and blasphemous prospect to a gospel-centered believer. But the fact is, every time you break the seventh commandment, you are joining Christ to that which is immoral, impure, defiled, and unholy.

A self-conscious understanding of the gospel and its implications, however, can fundamentally shape how you live each day. This will govern how you think, what you say, and how you act. This truly is *good news*! As Trisha now says, "We are learning how to rebuild our marriage on the foundation of Christ, learning how to be open and vulnerable again, and love each other more than ever."

The law can tell us what God forbids and requires, but only the gospel and its implications can motivate us to fulfill the law. We need a self-conscious realization of our union with Christ. That's why Paul asks the Corinthians twice in verses 15–17, "Do you not know?"

If we truly desire to flee sexual immorality and glorify God with our bodies, we must reflect afresh on our union with Christ and its implications for purity in our sexual lives. Every sexually immoral act by a believer joins Christ in that act. This is why sexual immorality cannot be justified as "lawful" (v. 12) or as simply the momentary satisfaction of a natural desire (v. 13a). The believer's body is joined to the Lord and becomes one in spirit with Him. Thus, the body is not meant for sexual immorality but for the Lord, and the Lord for the body.

There is much to consider here. Have you ever thought about how many times—by thought or action—you have joined Christ to sexual immorality? For many of us, the mountain of guilt would be overwhelming. And yet, though you are exceedingly guilty, all this sin is not held against you! This good news is shocking and seemingly too good to be true.

How can this be? How can God, time after time, forgive us for polluting His Son? As we have seen, Paul has already given us the answer in verse 11:

> And such were some of you. But you were washed, you were sanctified, you were justified in the name of the Lord Jesus Christ and by the Spirit of our God.

All who are in Christ have been *washed*—regenerated and cleansed from not only their past sins but also the present and all future sins. All who are in Christ have been *sanctified*, chosen and set apart by God for God to be saints/holy ones. All who are in Christ have been *justified* and declared righteous and perfect law-keepers. Because we have been justified, our sexual sins and failures—though unspeakably wicked and defiling—are not held against us!

In my ecclesiastical tradition, we recite the Apostles' Creed twice a day at Morning and Evening Prayer. In article three of the Creed, we confess, "I believe in . . . the forgiveness of sins." By this, we are reminded twice daily that all our sins and failures are not held against us. Question 56 in the Heidelberg Catechism asks, "What do you believe concerning 'the forgiveness of sins'?" Here is the comforting answer, "That God, for the sake of Christ's satisfaction, will no more remember my sins, nor the sinful nature with which I have to struggle all my life long; but graciously imputes to me the righteousness of Christ, that I may nevermore come into condemnation."[23]

My friend Peter had struggled for years with sexual fantasies, an addiction to pornography, and masturbation. After making a decision for Christ in childhood, he latched onto purity culture but found it brought no power in overcoming his sexual sin. Outwardly, he was lauded for maintaining a pure lifestyle, but Peter knew the truth. Eventually he married a fine Christian woman, but even a happy marriage did not tame his unholy urges.

Eventually Peter came to a church where God's Word for all of life is taught and began to learn how a true understanding of the gospel could deliver him from sexual bondage. "My whole life, I could never fully believe my hideous sin could be truly and completely forgiven by God," he said. "It wasn't until I truly and completely stopped relying on my own strength, which had no power to overcome any temptation, and asked Christ, who lived perfectly for me and had all the power for salvation to overcome through me, did I experience freedom over the bondage of sexual sin and shame."

Such forgiving grace, of course, doesn't justify our sins or provide a license to indulge in them. Rather, as it did with Peter, it leads us to repentance and confession and an active pursuit of purity and disciplined living (both inside and outside the marriage bond). Moreover, such saving actions by God testify to the unfathomable, unspeakable grace of God in Christ toward us.

Because of your sexual sin, you might find yourself crying out like Paul (or Peter), "Wretched man that I am! Who will deliver me from this body of death?" (Rom. 7:24; see Luke 5:8). If so, learn to turn from yourself and your failures and look to Christ and confess, "Thanks be to God through Jesus Christ our Lord!" (Rom. 7:25). Though the law continually reveals our most obvious and basic problem—sin—the gospel continually provides our only remedy for our sin—Jesus Christ, and our union with Him.

Chapter 7

OUR BODIES ARE TEMPLES OF THE HOLY SPIRIT

THE CORINTHIAN BELIEVERS knew all about temples. Frank Thielman writes, "In Paul's day the great Doric-style temple (to Athena or Apollo) from the sixth century BC remained a central feature in Corinth, and multiple temples to other deities dotted the city."[1] The famous Greek temple of Aphrodite (the Greek goddess of sexual love and beauty, identified with Venus by the Romans),[2] which stood at the top of Acrocorinth ("upper Corinth"), had been rebuilt by the Romans. Though this rebuilt Roman temple didn't really house a thousand temple prostitutes as some have claimed, licentious sexual immorality nevertheless would have been common at such a port city as Corinth.[3]

The problem with some of the male converts in the Corinthian church is that they were being influenced by the prevailing cultural mores from which they had been saved.[4] D. A. Carson and Douglas Moo write, "Their Christian faith, however sincere, had not yet transformed the worldview they had adopted from the surrounding culture. They had not grasped how the theology of the cross not only constitutes the basis of our salvation but also and inevitably teaches us how to live and serve."[5]

Consequently, some were arguing for their "right" to frequent prostitutes (1 Cor. 6:15–17; see 1 Cor. 6:12–13, 18, for the theological slogans used to justify their so-called right.).[6]

Clearly, the gospel and its implications had not sunk in. These Corinthian men were guilty of idolatry. As we saw in chapter 3, sexual immorality and idolatry go together. Let's imagine Paul directing their attention to the multiple temples to other deities that dotted the city and saying in exasperation,

> Do you not know? The temple of Apollo, which is idolatry, is not where the presence of the living God dwells. Do you not know that sex with a prostitute is idolatry? There are not *many* gods. There is only *one* God, and He, by His Holy Spirit, dwells in you. You cannot desecrate God's temple (your body) and join yourself in an unholy union with a prostitute. The indwelling presence of the Holy Spirit marks you off as God's people—His temple—in Corinth.

Paul is telling the Corinthians that there is only one temple in the city, and they are it, both corporately and individually![7] In chapter 3, verses 16–17, Paul applies the temple imagery to the church as a whole.

> Do you not know that you are God's temple and that God's Spirit dwells in you? If anyone destroys God's temple, God will destroy him. For God's temple is holy, and you are that temple.

In these verses, the Greek word translated as "you" is plural. When the church is gathered corporately in Jesus' name, He is in the midst of His people. Paul issues a chilling warning against anyone who would seek to destroy God's dwelling place—the church. In 1 Corinthians 5:4, Paul again confirms that Jesus is present among His people and that He endorses the disciplinary action of the church against unrepentant professing members of the church.[8]

God's promised presence with His people is the essence of the one covenant of grace.[9] God's covenant promise runs from Genesis to Revelation and unifies redemptive history.[10] God first made this promise to Abraham (Gen. 17:7). Four hundred years later, God makes this same promise to the biological descendants of Abraham when He delivers them from slavery in Egypt (Ex. 6:7).[11] And millennia later, God's promise is found in the New Testament as Paul applies it to the Corinthian believers in Corinth:

"What agreement has the temple of God with idols? For we are the temple of the living God; as God said, 'I will make my dwelling among them and walk among then, and I will be their God, and they shall be my people'" (2 Cor. 6:16). Finally, as we come to the concluding chapters of Revelation, we find the consummation of God's covenant promise recorded in John's vision of a new heaven and earth (Rev. 21:2–3).[12]

In 1 Corinthians 6:19a Paul applies the truth of God's presence among His people to the individual believer:

Or do you not know that your body is a temple of the Holy Spirit within you?

The Corinthians became God's temple in Corinth at regeneration ("washed," 1 Cor. 6:11). Yet they were arrogantly tolerating and living in unrestrained sexual license. This put the witness of God's presence in the city at risk. Fee writes, "As God's temple in Corinth, the church was to be his alternative to Corinth, both its religions and vices. But the Corinthians, by their worldly wisdom, boasting, and divisions, were in effect 'banishing' the Spirit and thus about to destroy the only alternative God had in their city."[13]

119

Tabernacle/Temple Imagery

The temple imagery was not just familiar to the Corinthians, of course. For Paul, the temple imagery was rooted in the Old Testament and thus was deeply rich in meaning and significance. In a Jewish context, temple imagery would immediately lead to thoughts of God dwelling with His people—a theme, as just noted, that winds its way throughout the Bible.

The garden of Eden was the first dwelling place of God with His people (Gen. 2:9–14). "Eden," writes Daniel Hyde, "was adorned with beauty as the temple of God, the first true Holy Land, anticipating Israel's tabernacle and later its temple (Ex. 25:3, 7; 1 Kings 6:20–22, 28, 30, 32, 35)."[14]

> **The tabernacle was situated at the center of Israel's camp as the sacred space where God dwelled in the midst of His people.**

But having broken God's covenant, Adam and Eve were banished from God's presence and sent out into bondage east of Eden. But God, who is the God of promise and performance, immediately promises (speaks a word of grace and the gospel) to once again dwell in the midst of His people (Gen. 3:15).

In partial fulfillment of this initial promise, as well as the Abrahamic covenant, God redeemed His people from slavery in Egypt.

Next, God revealed His instructions to Moses for building the tabernacle (Ex. 25:1–31:11) and then led him to write an inspired account of its construction (Ex. 35:4–40:38).[15] The tabernacle was to serve as the Lord's dwelling place during Israel's forty-year wilderness journey and their first three hundred-plus years in Canaan. The tabernacle was referred to by several different names. It was called "the sanctuary" (Ex. 25:8; 38:24), since it was the place of the holy presence of

God. It was also called the "tent of meeting" (Ex. 27:21; 30:20; 40:32; Num. 8:24), since it was where the Lord met with His people.

The tabernacle was situated at the center of Israel's camp as the sacred space where God dwelled in the midst of His people. Following the tabernacle era, David expressed a desire to build a house for God (2 Sam. 7:1–3). Yet God told David that he would not build a house for the Lord but rather would *receive* a house from the Lord (2 Sam. 7:8–17). In Deuteronomy 12, God says six times that He will "choose" the place where His Name will dwell (Deut. 12:5, 11, 14, 18, 21, 26). This is why God, not David, would choose both the place and the builder. And so God promises David, in the Davidic covenant, that the king will have a son—Solomon—who will build a temple and whose throne will be established forever (2 Sam. 7:4–12). God's dwelling among His people is a matter of promise and grace, not merit and work. It is an indescribable privilege.[16] As with the tabernacle, the temple was the centerpiece within the promised land. Among other things, it served as a witness to Israel and the nations that God dwells in the midst of His people (1 Kings 8:41–43). When the ark—which symbolized the Lord's presence and which contained the tablets of the law—was brought into the temple, the glory of the Lord filled it (1 Kings 8:1–11).

Following the glorious temple era of David and Solomon, the nation plummets into destruction and exile, just as the Lord warned in the Mosaic covenant (Deut. 28:36ff). In Ezekiel 10:18, the prophet tells us that God executes the worst of all covenant curses: the glory and presence of the Lord leave the temple. God's presence goes to the east gate of the temple, thus typologically recalling how Adam and Eve had been banished east of Eden, away from the presence of the Lord (Gen. 3:23–24).[17] And so the temple was left *ichabod*, without glory (1 Sam. 4:19–22).

When God's people return from captivity, they rebuild the temple (see Ezra, Nehemiah, and Haggai). Yet the Second Temple not only pales in comparison with the First Temple, but it—along with the tabernacle and First Temple—is only a faint "copy and shadow" of "the Temple" that is to come.[18]

He Tabernacled among Us

Then, after four hundred silent years, God comes again to dwell among His people. In John 1:14, we read, "And the Word became flesh and *dwelt* among us, and we have seen his glory, glory as of the only Son from the Father, full of grace and truth." The word "dwelt" (*eskēnōsen*) literally means "pitched His tent." In other words, Jesus "tabernacled" among us. John is unequivocally stating that Jesus is the fulfillment of the tabernacle and temple—God's dwelling among His people.

In times past, God temporarily dwelled among His people in the tabernacle and temple. But now He comes to dwell among His people as the incarnate Word, Jesus Christ. Just as God's glory filled the temple when the Israelites brought the ark into it, so John says that "we have seen his glory, glory as of the only Son from the Father, full of grace and truth" (John 1:14). The author of Hebrews in 8:5 and 10:1 says that the coming of Jesus was the fulfillment of the Old Testament shadows.

In the Gospels, Christ promised His disciples that He would send His Spirit to dwell with His people (Matt. 28:20; John 14:16–17). As the ascended, conquering King, Jesus dispenses the spoils of His victory and sends the Holy Spirit to dwell in the midst of His people (Acts 2). The coming of the Holy Spirit makes God's people into a temple, both corporately when they are assembled (1 Cor. 3:16, "God's Spirit dwells in you"; Matt. 18:15–20) and individually (the believer's body becomes God's temple; 1 Cor. 6:19).

While the tabernacle and temple served as copies and shadows, now the fulfillment has come through Christ. Furthermore, because the church is in union with Christ, the Temple (1 Cor. 6:15–17), they too become a temple (v. 19a)! Thus, Paul writes in Ephesians 2:19–22, "So then you [Gentiles] are no longer strangers and aliens, but you are fellow citizens with the saints [Jews], and members of the household of God, been built on the foundation of the apostles and prophets, Christ Jesus himself being the cornerstone, in whom the whole structure, being joined together, grows into a holy temple in the Lord. In him you also are being built together into a dwelling place for God by the Spirit."

A New Temple in Town

Paul is driving home a powerful point: through the indwelling gift of the Holy Spirit, the Corinthians are God's temple in the city, where each member also constitutes the holy dwelling place of God. Since the believer's body is now and forevermore the temple of the Holy Spirit (a dwelling place for God), he or she must not defile it by engaging in sexual immorality (see Rev. 21:22–27). The old pagan sexual ethic of Corinth must give way to the new sexual ethic of God's kingdom. There is a new temple in town.

Having sexual relations with a prostitute was not counted a consecration but rather a desecration of God's true temple. Sexual immorality is appalling idolatry, which leads to defilement and disgrace ("put to shame . . . . put to shame . . . . put to shame," see Isa. 44:9, 11). Just as it was unthinkable to desecrate and disgrace the tabernacle or temple, so it is unthinkable that the believer would desecrate and disgrace his or her own body, which is now the temple of the Holy Spirit.

Let us look carefully at verses 18–20 of 1 Corinthians 6 to see what other insights we may glean in the struggle against sexual immorality.

Flee sexual immorality! "Every sin a person commits is outside of the body"—but the immoral person sins against his own body. Or do you not know that your body is the temple of the Holy Spirit who is in you, whom you have from God, and you are not your own? For you were bought at a price. Therefore glorify God with your body.[19]

If you're familiar with the English Standard Version, New American Standard Bible, and New International Version translations, you may have noticed that the word "other" is missing from the portion above that reads "Every sin a person commits." That's because the word "other" is not in the Greek text.[20] The New English Translation, the American Standard Version, and the King James Version are preferable because they leave it out.

As a reminder, throughout 1 Corinthians 6:12–20 Paul has been correcting the Corinthians' erroneous theological slogans, which they were using to justify *engaging in* rather than *fleeing from* sexual immorality (vv. 12–13). Here in verses 18–20, Paul deals with one final slogan.[21] The dialogue goes like this:

> *Paul's command:* "Flee sexual immorality!"
> *Corinthians' slogan/objection:* [But why?] "Every sin a person commits is outside of the body."
> *Paul's reply:* "But the sexually immoral person sins against his own body."[22]
> *Paul's proof:* "Or do you not know that your body is a temple of the Holy Spirit within you, whom you have from God? You are not your own, for you were bought with a price."
> *Paul's conclusion:* "So glorify God in your body."

As we have seen, the Corinthians were under the influence of Greek dualism. They believed that the physical body is morally insignificant and therefore cannot be used as an instrument of sin (sin was "outside of [*ektos*] the body"). Paul rebuts, "but the immoral person sins against his own body." After arguing in verses 15–17 that the believer who commits sexual immorality sins against Christ's body (i.e., dishonors and defiles the body of Christ), now, in verse 18, Paul states that the believer who commits sexual immorality sins against his or her own body. Great damage then is done not only against Christ's body but

also the believer's body (see 1 Cor. 6:12a, "not all things are helpful").
Let's take a closer look at Paul's command in verse 18a, "flee from
sexual immorality." It means "to keep from doing something by avoiding it because of its potential damage, flee from, avoid, shun."[23] Paul
has already addressed the destructive nature of sexual immorality in
6:12a ("not all things are helpful"). His command has been inherent
throughout his entire argument. But, now in verse 18, he issues the
exhortation clearly and forcefully.[24]

Because the danger of sexual immorality is ever present, Paul's
command is in the present tense. Avoiding sexual immorality is to be
an ongoing daily moral imperative of the believer. The question is *how*?
How do we, daily immersed in sexual temptations in a sex-obsessed
culture, continually avoid it? It is not by fear or slavish attempts to
obey the law. We must avail ourselves of the Spirit.

Paul asks the Corinthians, "Or do you not know that your body is
a temple of the Holy Spirit within you, whom you have from God?" It
is clear that they did *not* know. They had forgotten the work of Christ
for us (the gospel) as well as the work of Spirit *in us* (the fruit of the
gospel; see Gal. 3:14). They had missed a cardinal implication (fruit)
of the gospel: the believer's body belongs to the Lord because it is a
sacred temple of the Holy Spirit. The believer's body is a holy habitation of the Lord and is therefore not meant for sexual immorality, but
for the Lord, and the Lord for the body.

REFLECTION

As we reflect on Paul's teaching that every believer is a temple of the
Holy Spirit, we learn a vital truth about sexual purity: *The path to
sexual purity is paved by self-consciously contemplating the implications
of being God's temple—the dwelling place of the Holy Spirit.*

In his work *On the Trinity*, Saint Augustine wrote, "There is no
greater gift of God than the Holy Spirit."[25] Likewise, Robert Murray

M'Cheyne said the gift of the Holy Spirit is God's "greatest of all the privileges of a Christian."[26] God is determined to take up residence in His temple and dwell with His people. We learned this from 2 Samuel 7 and God's everlasting covenant with David. Such grace moves us to obedience.

Calvin writes, "It is a great honour that God confers upon us when He desires to dwell in us . . . Psalm 132:14."[27] The Holy Spirit—God's empowering[28] and purifying presence among His people—is the source of gospel holiness. In the battle for sexual purity, the church must recapture this gospel-centered vision of what it means to be the temple of the Holy Spirit by God's grace.

Not surprisingly, the Holy Spirit comes to dwell in believers to make us *holy* (in this context, conformed to the sexual ethic of God's kingdom). As citizens of that kingdom, we have been regenerated and indwelt by the Holy Spirit (1 Cor. 6:9–11).

The Spirit leads us to live by a separate code of ethics—kingdom ethics (i.e., fulfillment of the seventh commandment, see also Matt. 5:27–30; Eph. 5:3; 1 Thess. 4:3). Thus, we are to be God's alternative to both our culture's religions and immoral ethics.

To be sure, believers need to live holier lives, particularly in regard to sexual sins. Yet progress in holiness does not depend on self-effort. The ultimate responsibility for sanctification belongs to the Holy Spirit (see 2 Thess. 2:13; 1 Peter 1:2), which is why we need to diligently ask God for the grace of the Holy Spirit, that we may be renewed more and more after God's image, until we attain the goal of perfection after this life.[29]

It is important to keep in mind that our progress in holiness (albeit a small beginning in this life)[30] is the fruit of the Holy Spirit's gracious sanctifying work. Question 35 in the Westminster Shorter Catechism reminds us that sanctification is "the work of God's free grace, whereby we are renewed in the whole man after the image of God, and are enabled more and more to die unto sin, and live unto righteousness."[31] Nevertheless, while sanctification is the Holy Spirit's work of grace, let us not fail to note how the catechism says that believers are enabled by the Holy Spirit to more and more die unto sin, and live unto righteousness.[32] Consequently, believers can (and must) flee from, avoid, and shun sexual immorality.

In a message preached at Saint Peter's in 1837 on Romans 8:13, M'Cheyne spoke of the need to "mortify the deeds of the body." He asked, "How are we to do this?" His answer: "It is through the Spirit— this is the secret of gospel holiness; never forget it." He then went on to speak of the "fire" of sin, saying, "The only way to put out the fire is to let in the water of the Spirit."[33]

What does it mean to let in the water of the Holy Spirit? Few temptations prove more overwhelming than sexual sin. In 1 Corinthians 7:9, Paul speaks of sexual temptation as burning with passion. As one author writes, "This powerful fire is easily lit and very difficult to extinguish."[34] We extinguish it by living with a self-conscious awareness that our bodies are temples of the Holy Spirit (i.e., the dwelling place of a holy God). Aware of this truth, we won't desecrate our bodies with sexual immorality. We also keep before us the exhortation of God's law, to "flee sexual immorality."

As Spirt-indwelt believers, we will be directed by God's law ("flee," v. 18, and "glorify," v. 20) and driven by the gospel and the Holy Spirit to consecrate our bodies. Sexually immoral passion cannot burn in a river of gospel love poured out in our hearts by the Holy Spirit.[35]

A gospel-driven perspective constantly informs us that our bodies are "a sacred shrine indwelt by the Spirit of God" and belong to the Lord rather than sexual immorality.[36] The Spirit's temple-building work is based completely on the work of Christ, who has sent His Spirit to His church to grow us into a holy temple in the Lord. Paul says God the Father has sent Christ into the world to redeem us (v. 20a), and He has sent the Spirit of His Son into our hearts to indwell and sanctify us (v. 19a; see Gal. 4:4–6).

> **We have been brought into union with Jesus, and the Holy Spirit communicates Him and all His saving benefits to us.**

The gospel is the ministry of the Holy Spirit (2 Cor. 3:8). The Holy Spirit uses the gospel to motivate us to live holy lives by leading us in gospel love rather than driving us with legal fear. The law is the ministry of condemnation, but the gospel is the ministry of righteousness (2 Cor. 3:9).

In a sermon titled "The Love of Christ," M'Cheyne states, "No man was ever frightened into love, and therefore, no man was ever frightened into holiness." M'Cheyne thus concludes that God has "invented a way of drawing us to holiness. By showing us the love of his Son, he calleth forth our love."[37] The apostle John says it like this, "We love because he first loved us" (1 John 4:19). How did God first love us? John writes, "In this the love of God was made manifest among us, that God has sent his only Son into the world, so that we might live through him. In this is love, not that we have loved God but that he loved us and sent his Son to be the propitiation for our sins" (1 John 4:9–10).

We have been brought into union with Jesus, and the Holy Spirit communicates Him and all His saving benefits to us. The third person of the Trinity leads us to Christ and through the gospel shines the love of Christ like a floodlight into our hearts, thereby assuring us of the Father's good pleasure and favor toward us. This is the source and path of holiness. Marshall writes,

> God does not drive you along with whips and terrors or by the rod of the schoolmaster, the law. Rather, he leads you and draws you to walk in his ways by pleasant attractions (Hosea

11:3–4). The love of Christ, of course, is the greatest and most pleasant attraction to encourage you to godly living (2 Cor. 5:15; Rom. 12:1).[38]

But of course, Paul understands that when the alluring power of Christ's gospel love fails to motivate us to holiness, we need to hear the warning of God's law.[39] Question 115 of the Heidelberg Catechism asks, "No one in this life can obey the Ten Commandments perfectly: Why then does God want them preached so pointedly?" Here's the answer:

> First, so that the longer we live the more we may come to know our sinfulness and the more eagerly look to Christ for forgiveness of sins and righteousness. Second, so that, while praying to God for the grace of the Holy Spirit, we may never stop striving to be renewed more and more after God's image, until after this life we reach our goal: perfection.[40]

Nonetheless, while the law has a critical role to play in the believer's life, "God," Calvin writes, "breathes faith into us only by the instrument of his gospel, as Paul points out that 'faith comes from hearing and hearing by the word of Christ' [i.e., the gospel; Rom. 10:17]."[41] The gospel is the ministry of the Holy Spirit (2 Cor. 3:8). As the Holy Spirit breathes faith into us by the ministry of the gospel, our faith produces good works and obedience (including obeying the seventh commandment and living by the ethics of the kingdom). This work of the Spirit fulfills what was prophesied by Ezekiel concerning the new covenant:

> "I will sprinkle clean water on you, and you shall be clean from all your uncleannesses, and from all your idols I will cleanse you. And I will give you a new heart, and a new spirit

I will put within you. And I will remove the heart of stone from your flesh and give you a heart of flesh. And I will put my Spirit within you, and cause you to walk in my statutes and be careful to obey my rules." (Ezek. 36:25–27)

So how should we respond to the truth that our bodies are temples of the Holy Spirit?

1. We will live with a self-conscious awareness that our bodies are a holy temple of the Holy Spirit. As those who are indwelt by the Holy Spirit, we will guard ourselves from the defiling idol of sexual immorality (1 John 5:21). We will keep ourselves away from all sexual immorality (flee) and live as disciplined, holy vessels, fit for the Lord's service in His church so that we might glorify God in our bodies.
2. We will constantly pray to God, as the Heidelberg Catechism states (Q. 115), for the grace of the Holy Spirit to transform us more and more into the image of Jesus Christ.[42]
3. We will hunger and thirst to experience the love of God in Jesus Christ as we meditate on the gospel and the fruit of the gospel (i.e., the indwelling, empowering, purifying presence of the Holy Spirit).

Assurance of God's love is the source and power for a holy life. Walter Marshall writes,

You cannot love God if you are under the continual, secret suspicion that he is really your enemy! You cannot love God if you secretly think he condemns and hates you. This kind of slavish fear will compel you to some hypocritical obedience— such as what Pharaoh did when he let the Israelites go against his will. However, you will never truly love God if you are compelled only by fear. Your love for God must be won and drawn out by your understanding of God's love and goodness towards you.[43]

We only know how much the Father loves us through the gospel, which is the ministry of the Holy Spirit. And so the Holy Spirit— God's empowering and purifying presence among His people—is the source of gospel holiness. Praise God, providing the power for holiness is *His* work, not ours!

Chapter 8

OUR BODIES WERE BOUGHT BY CHRIST ON THE CROSS

SHARON WAS BRUTALLY HONEST. "We'd been married for fifteen years, and a perfect storm was brewing," she said. "I didn't know if my marriage would last another day, let alone another year, decade, or lifetime. I felt alienated and rejected by my husband. He was living his own life. Drinking. Spending time alone. Not engaging with the family. Not 'completing' me. I used these feelings of alienation as kindling to fuel my bitterness."

And she also used these feelings of alienation as an excuse to begin an affair with an old flame. In the midst of the affair, however, Sharon knew what she was doing was wrong, yet she had no power to become the person she had thought she was in Christ. So she cried out to the Lord.

> For three years after the affair, I lived in sorrow, regret, and utter disbelief at what I had done and what I had become. I was just a shadow of who I thought I was. I wanted to die. I

had visions of slitting my wrists, cutting my veins, and bleeding out. I would never have attempted suicide, not that way at least. This whole cluster of events was a demonic attack. If I didn't know it in the beginning, I knew it then. So I cried out to God, again and again, "Change me! I cannot change myself! Change me or take me out of this life." I had ruined it and turned my back on all that was good in it. I remembered the gospel but was not altogether certain that God was not angry and turning His back to me because of what I had done.

In giving her body and her emotions to another man, Sharon had forgotten the strict but freeing truth that her body is a temple of the Spirit, the gift of a God who loved her deeply. Perhaps if she had remembered, a lot of heartache could have been avoided.

We encountered the glorious and freeing truth in the last chapter that the believer's body is a sacred temple because of the indwelling presence of the Holy Spirit. An important gospel implication of this truth is, "Your bodies are not your own to do with whatever you desire sexually." To further drive home the point, Paul gives another gospel-centered argument.

By now it shouldn't surprise us that Paul is directing us one final time to the gospel. He began this section of 1 Corinthians 6 (vv. 12–20) by appealing to the resurrection—the hope of the gospel (vv. 12–14). The great apostle concludes it by appealing to the death of Christ on the cross—the heart of the gospel. Paul is pointing the Corinthians (and us!) to what is to be paramount in our lives.

As we have seen, the gospel is God's power to save (Rom. 1:16). This includes not just going to heaven when we die but also the whole process of sanctification and glorification. Remember that salvation for the Christian is a three-dimensional ministry of the Holy Spirit, with a past ("I have been saved," Eph. 2:5, 8), a present ("I am being saved," Titus 2:11–14), and a future ("I will be saved," Rom. 5:9).

The Holy Spirit uses the gospel to bring us into conformity to the requirements of God's law. This is the work of God's free grace, whereby we are renewed in wholeness after the image of God and are enabled more and more to die unto sin and live unto righteousness.[1] In this context, doing so means that we will "flee from sexual immorality," verse 18, and "glorify God in your body," verse 20. Paul is teaching us that "we do not move on from the milk of the Gospel to the meat of something else, but from the milk of the Gospel to the meat of the Gospel."[2] Self-conscious gospel-centrality assures and motivates us toward sexual purity.

As Paul now closes his argument for sexual purity, he directs us to the heart of the gospel—the cross of Christ. The indwelling presence of the Holy Spirit and Christ's redemption on the cross are God's affirmation of the believer's body. We belong to God not only by right of habitation but also by redemption.

REDEMPTION: PURCHASED POSSESSION OF CHRIST (VV. 19B–20A)

As I and many others have noted, the cross is at the heart of the gospel. When Jesus died for us as the one and only substitutionary sacrifice for our sins, He "bought" us at a price. Paul writes in verses 19 and 20, "You are not your own, for you were bought with a price." The price was Christ's death. The purpose of Christ's death is multifaceted. The aspect Paul focuses on here is redemption. Paul moves from temple imagery in verse 19a to that of the slave market in verse 20a.

Now, like the temple imagery, the slavery imagery is exceedingly rich. Referencing a slave market would have been an immediately meaningful image to the Corinthians. Corinth was a major center for slave trafficking.[3] In fact, modern historians note that "sacred prostitutes" of Corinth were most likely "slaves purchased by wealthy Greeks and dedicated to the temple as a form of religious offering."[4]

Apparently there were even "bondservants" in the Corinthian congregation (1 Cor. 7:21–24).[5]

In Paul's day, a price would be paid in the marketplace to purchase a slave. Paul carries over this idea through the use of the word "bought" (*ēgorasthēte*), which means "to secure the rights to someone by paying a price, buy, acquire as property."[6] It was used for "an ordinary transfer of ownership" and pictures a slave being sold from one owner to another.[7] Paul's imagery raises an important question: To whom was Christ's payment paid?

Paul doesn't say. A widespread interpretation during the Middle Ages held that Christ paid a price to the devil, that is, His sacrificial death was in effect a ransom paid to Satan. If this were true, there would be a sense in which Satan triumphed over Christ, when in fact the opposite is true.[8] Further, we must not think of Christ's payment as a literal monetary exchange paid to Satan. Otherwise, as Jerry Bridges notes, Satan would be laughing all the way to the bank.[9]

Paul's use of this word must be understood figuratively. When Jesus died on the cross, He paid the price for His people. Peter says, "you were ransomed from the futile ways inherited from your forefathers, not with perishable things such as silver or gold, but with the precious blood of Christ, like that of a lamb without blemish or spot" (1 Peter 1:18–19). Leon Morris writes, "Christ's blood is at one and the same time the offering of a sacrifice which avails for men, and the payment of a price which avails for men. We are atoned for and we are purchased."[10]

In chapter 6, verses 9–10, Paul reminds the Corinthians that prior to their conversion they were in bondage to sin, which was their master. Prior writes, "They were slaves to themselves, their self-centered desires, self-indulgence and bodily passions." But Jesus, by dying on the cross, paid the necessary price to set them free from their former manner of life. Prior adds, "Their bodies were no longer like chunks of flesh up for sale to the highest bidder in the slave-market. . . . They had been bought with a price and they now belonged to a new master."[11]

Thus, by paying a price, Christ frees us from our former way of life, which is characterized as bondage to sin. Still, the question remains: To whom was Christ's payment made? Elsewhere, the Scriptures reveal that it was paid to God acting in His capacity of Judge.[12] Jesus satisfied God's justice on the cross. Paul writes in Galatians

> **The purpose of Christ's redemption is not merely to set us free, but to allow us to *belong to God* in covenant relationship.**

3:13, "Christ redeemed us from the curse of the law by becoming a curse for us—for it is written, 'Cursed is everyone who is hanged on a tree'" (see Gal. 4:4–5).

Now, while Christ's redemption certainly results in the believer's freedom from the curse of God's law, as well as his or her former manner of life, the emphasis in this context is more on *ownership*. The purpose of Christ's redemption is not merely to set us free, but to allow us to *belong to God* in covenant relationship.

Figuratively speaking, Paul says Christ died to purchase His people from slavery so that they can belong to Him. Through the gospel, God restores His presence in the midst of His people. After the resurrection, Jesus told His disciples to wait for the promise of the Father (the coming of the Holy Spirit; Luke 24:49). By the indwelling Spirit, God's people once more experience His presence. In the Spirit, Jesus comes and is present with His people. The Holy Spirit unites us to Christ both corporately (1 Cor. 3:16–17) and individually (1 Cor. 6:19a). And so, we have been freed from our enslavement to our former master so that we might now belong to a new Master, who dwells within us!

Christ's death has sealed a transfer of ownership. Christ "bought" and secured the rights to believers by paying the price with His blood—death on the cross. So Jesus now has "full property rights over [His people.] . . . God has the title deed to their bodies," Garland writes. "Christ's death purchased them, and they have been transferred from Satan's household to serve in Christ's household. It brings improved status, new duties, and increased accountability."[13]

Yes, belonging to God implies responsibility, not license. Keep in mind that Paul is confronting and correcting the Corinthians' theological slogans, which they were using to justify *engaging in* rather than *fleeing from* sexual immorality. In reply to their slogan in verse 18b about every sin being "outside the body," Paul argues that since God now has full property rights to the believer's body, he or she may not engage in sexual license. Rather, as a bondslave of Christ, the believer has a new Master.

Believers may no longer live by their self-indulgence and bodily passions. Because they belong to a new Master—Christ—they must follow His will for their lives (1 Thess. 4:3–8). Though applied in a different context, Paul, in Romans 14:7–8, writes, "For none of us lives to himself, and none of us dies to himself. For if we live, we live to the Lord, and if we die, we die to the Lord. So then, whether we live or whether we die, we are the Lord's."

When the gospel is central in our lives, we will live for the Lord, not ourselves. Rather than desecrating and disgracing God's temple, the believer will use his or her body to glorify God. He is Christ's servant because of Christ's death on the cross. The Christian does not belong to himself, but rather to Jesus, whom He confesses as Lord (owner).

THE SLAVE MARKET AND THE PAULINE (JEWISH) CONTEXT

Paul's understanding of Christ's work of redemption was rooted in the Old Testament Scriptures. In our passage there may be an allusion to Hosea 3,[14] where Hosea "bought" (*hrk*, Hos. 3:2) his adulterous wife,

Gomer, out of slavery. The prophet redeems her from a sexually immoral lifestyle so that she will belong to him in a loving, monogamous marriage—one that depicts Israel's relationship with the Lord. Like Hosea, the Lord pursues Israel, the adulteress. God calls Hosea to retrieve his adulterous wife so that Israel will clearly know that the Lord still loves Israel, His spiritually unfaithful wife.[15]

In the same way, Christ redeemed the Corinthians from bondage to their sexually licentious lifestyle so that they might belong to Him and live in a way that glorifies Him.[16] Again, we see how possession marks the covenant relationship. God redeems His people so that He may possess them. By His redemption, Christ fulfills God's covenant promise: "You shall be my people, and I will be your God" (Gen. 17:7; Jer. 31:33; Ezek. 37:26–27).

This covenant promise is the essence of the covenant of grace.[17] As we have seen, the Lord's covenant promise runs from Genesis (17:7) to Revelation (21:2–3), spanning all of redemptive history.[18] Paul applies God's covenant promise to the believers in Corinth (2 Cor. 6:16). As Paul made clear in his first letter, God has made their body—corporately and individually—the temple of the living God. God, by the Holy Spirit, dwells in the midst of His people. Therefore, believers are to cleanse themselves from all defilement of flesh and spirit, perfecting holiness in the fear of God (2 Cor. 7:1).

Christ's saving act of redemption on the cross also recalls the exodus, God's great act of redeeming His people from slavery in Egypt. Christopher Wright, in his book *The Mission of God: Unlocking the Bible's Grand Narrative*, notes:

If you had asked a devout Israelite in the Old Testament period "Are you redeemed?" the answer would have been a most definite yes. And if you had asked "How do you know?" you would be taken aside to sit down somewhere while your friend recounted a long and exciting story—the story of the exodus. For indeed it is the exodus that provided the primary model of God's idea of redemption, not just in the Old Testament but even in the New, where it is used as one of the keys to understanding the meaning of the cross of Christ.[19]

When the New Testament writers refer to Jesus as our redemption, they are looking back at the exodus. God redeemed His people from Egyptian slavery so that they would belong to Him. Because God remembers His covenant with Abraham (the gospel promise in the Old Testament; see Gal. 3:8), He instructs Moses to tell the people of Israel,

"I am the LORD, and I will bring you out from under the burdens of the Egyptians, and I will deliver you from slavery to them, and I *will redeem you* with an outstretched arm and with great acts of judgment. *I will take you to be my people, and I will be your God,* and you shall know that I am the LORD your God, who has brought you out from under the burdens of the Egyptians. *I will bring you into the land* that I swore to give to Abraham, to Isaac, and to Jacob. I will give it to you for a possession. I am the LORD." (Ex. 6:6–8)

Clearly, possession marks the covenant relationship. God's people are redeemed in order to belong to Him.

In Exodus 15, Moses and the people of Israel sing praises in response to God's deliverance from Pharaoh's army. In verse 13, they sing, "You have led in your steadfast love [*hesed*; covenant faithfulness] the people whom you have redeemed; you have guided them by your strength to your holy abode."

Note how God's redemption is based on His steadfast love—covenant faithfulness to uphold His promise made to Abraham (see Ex. 6:5; Gen. 12:1–3). In redemption, God always takes the initiative because of His steadfast love.

Also note He redeemed them in order to guide them to His holy abode—God's dwelling place, Canaan or the hill of Jerusalem where the temple would be built. Again, God redeems His people in order to restore them to His presence—to belong to Him. In Exodus 19:4, God says to Moses, "You yourselves have seen what I did to the Egyptians, and how I bore you on eagles' wings and *brought you to myself.*" God acts in order to possess His people.[20]

The entire book of Exodus concerns the Lord's presence—delivering, guiding, and then dwelling with His people.[21] John 1:14a—"And the Word became flesh and dwelt among us"—reveals how all this points to the coming of Christ, who is the fulfillment of God's saving acts in the Old Testament—"For all the promises of God find their Yes in him" (2 Cor. 1:20). Just as God redeemed His people from slavery in Egypt to belong to Him, so Christ redeemed His people from their slavery under the curse of the law to belong to Him. Jesus, meaning "Yahweh saves," is God present with His people to save them from their sins (Matt. 1:21). Jesus, "Immanuel," meaning God with us (Isa. 7:14), is present in saving action, just as He was present in saving action throughout the exodus narrative. In 1 Corinthians 1:30, Paul says that Christ has become "to us wisdom from God, righteousness and sanctification and *redemption.*"

> **The entire book of Exodus concerns the Lord's presence— delivering, guiding, and then dwelling with His people.**

To conclude this important point, we see that in Titus 2:14, Jesus "gave himself for us to redeem us from all lawlessness and to purify for himself *a people for his own possession* who are zealous for good works."

As well, in 1 Peter 2:9, the apostle Peter applies the Old Testament descriptive terms for ancient Israel in Exodus 19:5–6 to the New Testament church. He writes, "But you are a chosen race, a royal priesthood, a holy nation, *a people for [God's] own possession.*"

Clearly, the goal of God's redeeming acts is to possess His people (and vice versa). Such possession implies responsibility rather than license. Jesus "bought us" (i.e., paid the necessary price) so that we might become His rightful possession (1 Cor. 6:20). Therefore, because our bodies rightfully belong to God, we aren't free to do with them whatever we want. Rather, we are to obey—out of gratitude, not slavish duty!—our new Master, who has purchased us as His treasured possession.[22] Therefore, we must flee sexual immorality and glorify God in our bodies.

We might paraphrase Paul's argument this way:

> By virtue of His death, Christ purchased you for God, which means that your bodies are included in this purchase. And so you are not your own. Your bodies now belong to God. Therefore, you are not free to engage in unrestrained sexual license. God now owns you. You belong to Him, body and soul. You are His own possession—a sacred temple of the Holy Spirit. Therefore, you are called to zealously and joyfully carry out His purpose for your life. This means you must flee sexual immorality and use your bodies to glorify God.

REFLECTION

Your body is God's lawful possession by a double right: *habitation* and *redemption.* Therefore, the only logical thing to do is flee sexual immorality and use your mortal frame to glorify God. Knowing that your body is a temple of the Holy Spirit and the purchased possession of Christ will motivate you to use it in ways that glorify God instead of dishonoring Him. And so, we see that the gospel ("bought with a price") and its fruit ("a temple of the Holy Spirit") lead us to fulfill the very purpose for which we were created—to glorify God.

Do you know that your body is God's temple? Do you know that your body is not your own to do with sexually whatever you want? It is *God's* property—He purchased it! Do you live day by day with the knowledge that God *owns* you? Do you know that you are God's treasured possession? Do you know that He has the title deed to your body, which is in union with Jesus and is destined for resurrection? This is why you must avoid all sexual immorality. The goal of sexual purity is not to please yourself but to glorify God (v. 20b). The gospel always directs our attitudes and actions to glorify God rather than to dishonor Him.

As someone who is indwelt by the Holy Spirit and purchased by Christ, you now belong to God. You have a new Master. The gospel allures you to be subject to the lordship of Christ in every area of your life—including your sexuality.[23] The alluring power of the gospel creates in you a desire to flee sexual immorality (1 Cor. 6:18a) and to glorify God in your body (1 Cor. 6:20b). In his book *Divine Allurement*, Ashley Null writes, "Perhaps no one expressed the results of feeling the alluring nature of the Gospel better than Thomas Becon, Cranmer's chaplain."[24] Becon, writing to Cranmer, pens the following:

> As I may unfeignedly report unto you the affect of my heart, verily since that ye declared to us the goodness of God the Father toward us through Jesus Christ I have felt in my heart such an earnest faith and burning love toward God and his Word, that me think a thousand fires could not pluck me away from the love of him. I begin now utterly to condemn, despise, reject, cast away, and set at naught all the pleasures of this world, wherein I have so greatly rejoiced in times past. All the threats of God, all the displeasures of God, all the fires

and pains of hell could never before this day so allure me to the love of God, as you have now done by expressing unto me the exceeding mercy and unspeakable kindness of God toward us wretched sinners, insomuch that now from the very heart I desire to know what I may do, that by some means I may show again my heart to be full fired on the seeking of his glory. For I now desire nothing more than the advancement of His name.[25]

What you do with your body matters greatly, and not just for you or your spouse. It is God's lawful possession by both habitation (His Spirit lives there) and redemption (Christ purchased it). Restored one day in the resurrection, your body will live for eternity. How could you even *think* of soiling it now sexually?

A gospel-driven, Spirit-indwelt believer will not justify sinful behavior, giving false justifications such as "All things are lawful for me. . . . Food is meant for the stomach and the stomach for food—and God will destroy both one and the other. . . . Every sin a person commits is outside the body." Such lies are at odds with your new Master and Lord. They are at odds with the alluring power of the gospel. They are at odds with God's great purposes for you, seen in Christ's redemption and the Spirit's indwelling.

Do you not *know*?

Part 3

Who Is God?

1 CORINTHIANS 6:20B

Chapter 9

THE GOAL OF SEXUAL PURITY

AS WE HAVE SEEN, sexual immorality is a besetting sin in our society. Tragically, it is also a besetting sin of Christ's church, across every denomination and tradition. We have seen too many people, even prominent leaders, who have succumbed to the trap of sexual sin. We know this snare is wrong but seemingly cannot escape it—over and over again. Most of the solutions proffered are long on effort and self-discipline. As such, they are self-focused and therefore leave us pretty much helpless in avoiding or escaping sexual slavery.

This has happened because we've failed to appropriate the gospel way of holiness that is available to every believer in Jesus Christ. As we have seen throughout this book, sexual purity is the birthright of every Christian. But we will only experience it if, as the apostle Paul says in 1 Corinthians 6:9–20, we choose to be who we are.

Let's briefly review what we've learned before we consider the capstone in this encouraging passage. Remember that Paul frames his argument to us by repeatedly asking the question, "Do you not know?" Each appearance of this question causes us to reflect on a gospel truth (or an implication of the gospel) that gives us spiritual ammunition to shoot down the lies that lure us into sexual hell. We'll recap each one in turn.

1. Do you not know that the unrighteous will not inherit the kingdom of God? (vv. 9–11)

First, Paul warns us that those who live in habitual, unrepented sin will not enter God's kingdom. Such actions and attitudes clearly indicate that a person is not a new creation (i.e., a saint, a citizen of the kingdom of God). Having issued this chilling warning from the law in verses 9–10, Paul, in verse 11, immediately sets forth the comforting and motivating good news concerning those who *can* inherit the kingdom of God. He reaffirms the Corinthians' remarkable transformation and new status as citizens (saints) in God's kingdom by appealing to the good news of regeneration, definitive sanctification (election), justification, and adoption. Paul writes, "And such were some of you. But you were washed, you were sanctified, you were justified in the name of the Lord Jesus Christ and by the Spirit of our God."

2. Do you not know that your bodies belong to Christ because they are destined for resurrection? (vv. 12–14)

Second, in verses 12–14, Paul appeals to the doctrine of the resurrection, which is "the Father's 'Amen' to the finished work of Christ." The resurrection validates the moral importance of the physical body and confirms that the believer's body belongs to the Lord.

3. Do you not know that your bodies belong to Christ because they are in union with Him? (vv. 15–17)

Third, Paul appeals to the believer's union with Christ. Sexual immorality creates an unholy bond between Christ and the impure and defiled (desecrates Christ's body/members, *melos*).

4. Do you not know that your bodies belong to God because they are His rightful possession by habitation and redemption? (vv. 18–20a)

Fourth, in verses 18–20a, Paul reminds the Corinthians that they are God's rightful (lawful) possession. The Holy Spirit lives in me, and God owns me by virtue of Christ's death on the cross. Therefore, sexual immorality is simply unthinkable to the Christian who lives his or her life in light of the gospel.

These are all wonderful and motivating Christian realities, but we need to delve into the wonders of one final truth, which we touched on briefly in the last chapter—the glory of God. This is the truth that supports all the others.

What is the ultimate goal of sexual purity? Paul gives us the answer in 1 Corinthians 6:20b: "*So glorify God in your body.*"

The great purpose of every believer's life is not to satisfy the self but to glorify God. The Westminster Shorter Catechism reminds us in Question 1, "What is the chief end of man? A. Man's chief end is to glorify God, and to enjoy Him forever."[1] "The glory of God," writes Thomas Watson, "is a silver thread which must run through all our actions."[2] And as Paul states in 1 Corinthians 10:31, "So, whether you eat or drink, or whatever you do, do all to the glory of God."

What is God's glory? The answer is twofold.

First, it is the glory that He has in Himself. As light is to the sun, so glory is intrinsic and essential to the Godhead: Father, Son, and Holy Spirit. "Glory," writes Watson, "is the sparkling of the Deity; it is so co-natural to the Godhead, that God cannot be God without it."[3]

Second, it is the glory that is ascribed to God. Looked at from a human angle, God's glory is that which we ascribe to Him.[4] This is what Paul has in mind here in verse 20b. To "glorify God" means "to influence one's opinion about another so as to enhance the latter's reputation, praise, honor, extol."[5] We glorify God—we lift up His name and magnify Him in the eyes of others—when we submit to His will for our sexual lives. We dishonor God and bring reproach upon His name and church when we give ourselves to sexual immorality. Sexual immorality defames the gospel. It dishonors Christ's name and corrupts the purity of His church (see 1 Cor. 5:6).

The question before us then is, "How do you flee sexual immorality and glorify God in your body?" Paul teaches us how to glorify God in our body here in 1 Corinthians 6. Before we explore this truth, it will be helpful to briefly examine how we do *not* glorify God.

You do not glorify God by legal holiness.

What is legal holiness? It is the path of inauthentic Christian living. It consists merely of "forms, routines, and outward appearances, maintained from self-regarding motives."[6] I recently came across two articles responding to the problem of sexual sin and how to deal with it, both of which illustrate legal holiness. One focuses on church leaders and the other lists several ways to help a person break sexually sinful habits and avoid recurrences. Both articles are nearly identical in approach. They both offer helpful advice to overcome sexual sin. But helpful advice is sometimes nothing more than law, which imposes more expectations and demands as conditions for success.[7] There is no power to change in either one, because there is no gospel!

Sanctification does not consist merely in being told what to do, regardless of how practical the advice may seem. The approach the message in these articles takes is what Graeme Goldsworthy refers to as "naked law"—offering imperatives without grounding them in the indicatives of the gospel.[8] The idea is that what we really need is good advice, good instruction, a life coach who uses God's instruction manual—the Bible—to give us practical steps.

Yes, both articles touch on some wise counsel in regard to temptation and sexual sin. To be sure, God's law provides much needed wisdom for pursuing a moral life. But exhortations without the gospel are legalistic and ultimately useless. To paraphrase Goldsworthy,

> If we constantly tell people what they should do in order to get their lives in order, we place a terrible legalistic burden on them. Of course we should obey God; of course we should love him with all our heart, mind, soul, and strength. Of

course we should flee sexual immorality and glorify God in our body. The Bible tells us so. But if we ever give the impression that these things are possible to do on our own, not only do we make the gospel irrelevant, but we suggest that the law is in fact a lot weaker in its demands than it really is. Legalism demeans the law by reducing its standards to the level of our competence, such as "steps to avoid sexual sin."[9]

The "take these steps" approach is mere legal holiness (the pursuit of sexual purity from self-regarding motives). Thus, Goldsworthy proposes asking this question, "Is it possible to preach a Christian sermon [or write a Christian article on pursuing sexual purity] without mentioning Jesus?"[10]

The answer is *no!* The problem with a "take these steps" approach is that you could be a Mormon, Jew, Muslim, New Ager, or even an atheist and follow its precepts. There is nothing distinctively Christian about it. This approach, as well-intended as it is, leaves you without any power or hope to actually become sexually pure. Paul's teaching, on the other hand, could be adapted as: *Do you not know that law can do no more in sanctification than it could in justification?*

Law can only do what law can do: *command.* This basic function of the law never changes![11] The law cannot justify (Gal. 3:21), and the law cannot sanctify (Gal. 3:2–3; see Rom. 7:13–25). Whether law comes to us in the form of the Ten Commandments or as "steps to avoid sexual sin," such moral instruction can only reveal what our duty is. It can never compel our hearts to actually do it.

Living near the beach affords me opportunities to watch large cruise and naval ships navigate through the Atlantic. Sophisticated satellite navigation systems guide these enormous vessels, but they have no power to actually move them even an inch. In like manner, God's law provides the direction for our sexual lives but not the power. Ordering our daily lives around "steps to avoid sexual sin" is like trying to power a ship by the navigation system instead of the engine![12]

And what is the engine? The gospel of Jesus Christ! The nature of obedience to God's law means that you cannot obey unless you receive the comfort of the gospel. We must regularly have the gospel preached into us so that our faith is comforted and strengthened so that we can actually obey the law, which guides us in the path of sexual purity and warns us when we veer off course.[13]

The Holy Spirit uses this externally preached word of good news to drive us out of ourselves and conform us to Christ. The gospel is the ministry of the Spirit (2 Cor. 3:8), which the Spirit uses to establish our hearts in holiness and assure us of God the Father's good will toward us. The Spirit, working through the gospel, subdues our hearts to the law, strengthens our faith against temptation, and builds us up in grace, which Paul says trains us "to renounce ungodliness and worldly passions, and to live self-controlled, upright, and godly lives in the present age, waiting for our blessed hope, the appearing of the glory of our great God and Savior Jesus Christ" (Titus 2:12–13).

Here in 1 Corinthians 6, Paul is showing us that whenever we swerve from the gospel, we lapse into license (antinomianism), an error as destructive as legalism (nomism).[14] The Corinthians were claiming their "right" to indulge in sexual license. They didn't know the gospel and had not seriously considered its implications for daily life. We face the same danger. Only a continual immersion in the gospel will ensure that our lives are conformed to the sound doctrines that flow from it (see 1 Cor. 6:18a, 20b; Titus 2:10).

The gospel must remain central—of first importance in all things (1 Cor. 15:3). If we want to see purity grow in our hearts and lives, we must continually immerse ourselves in the gospel. So, in contrast to "legal holiness," Paul presents a radically different approach—gospel holiness.[15]

You glorify God by gospel holiness.

The term gospel holiness was "Puritan shorthand for authentic Christian living, which springs from love and gratitude to God."[16] Here in 1 Corinthians 6, Paul shows us that a truly Christian ethic— gospel holiness—is based on the understanding that "the indicative always generates, and is not generated by, the imperative."[17] More on the distinction between them in a moment.

Paul doesn't say, "Flee sexual immorality and glorify God in your body so that Christ might purchase you and the Spirit might indwell you." No! Paul says, "Because Christ has bought you and the Holy Spirit has come to indwell you to make you into a holy temple, flee sexual immorality and glorify God in your body!" Gospel holiness springs from gratitude to God; it flows from the gospel. Paul's exhortations arise out of the good news of God's grace in the gospel. They are not simple imperatives of Christian behavior (i.e., "naked law").[18]

Legal holiness is mere empty religion. The average person on the street thinks the purpose of religion is to make people better by offering practical, down-to-earth principles or tips for success.[19] Such an approach, however, is sustained by self-regarding motives rather than God-glorifying, Spirit-wrought desires that make the believer wholeheartedly willing and ready to live for God.[20]

Paul is not offering such legal (in other words, powerless) holiness. Rather, he is saying, "Be who you are!" Mere religion calls us to be something we are not. But, as we have seen, because of the gospel, God's law calls us to be who we already are in Christ!

Notice that Paul only issues *three imperatives* in 1 Corinthians 6:9–20, in contrast to the voluminous "take these steps" approach, which appears in much of evangelical teaching. His three imperatives are "do not be deceived" (*planasthe*, v. 9), "flee"[21] (*pheugete*, v. 18), and "glorify" (*doxasate*, v. 20).

But Paul immerses these three imperatives in a sea of indicatives— that is, realities showing what God has already done for us and in us.

Paul demonstrates how the three imperatives arise out of the gospel of grace. His indicatives, pointing to the gospel and its fruit, are:

"inherit" (implies adoption, vv. 9–10)

"washed" (regeneration, v. 11)

"sanctified" (definitive sanctification, v. 11)

"justified" (justification, v. 11)

"raised" (i.e., resurrection, v. 14)

"members of Christ . . . joined to the Lord" (union with Christ, vv. 15–17)

"temple of the Holy Spirit" (the fruit of the gospel as the work of Christ *in us*, v. 19a)

"bought" (redemption of Christ by substitutionary atonement, v. 20a).

Take careful note: Paul appeals to *eight* truths of the gospel and its fruits while issuing only *three* imperatives! "But, Paul," someone following the usual approach might ask, "where are the practical steps?"

No one disagrees that the Corinthian situation was a moral disaster and that these failing believers needed to be confronted and corrected. They were certainly acting unwisely (1 Cor. 1–2). But to these sinning, erring, misguided believers, Paul gives nearly three times as much gospel as he does law (i.e., calls to action).

And when Paul uses the law, he uses it *lawfully*, carefully grounding all three imperatives in the full redemptive work of Christ *for* us and then *in* us (i.e., "*for us*"; crucifixion, v. 20a, and resurrection, v. 14; and "*in us*"; the fruit of the gospel, the present indwelling work of the Holy Spirit, v. 19).[22] And, of course, we must not overlook that Paul appeals to the believer's union with Christ (vv. 15–17), which John

Murray calls "the central truth of the whole doctrine of salvation."[23]

The Holy Spirit takes all the work that Christ has done *for us* in history and comes to dwell *in us* and unite us to Christ. Therefore, in Christ, believers possess all of Christ and His saving benefits: adoption, regeneration, definitive sanctification, justification, resurrection, indwelling of the Spirit, and redemption. No wonder Paul says in Ephesians 1:3, "Blessed be the God and Father of our Lord Jesus Christ, who has blessed us in Christ with *every spiritual blessing*"!

This brings us to Paul's concluding imperative in verse 20b, "So glorify God in your body." Like "flee" in verse 18, this command grows out of the rich gospel soil of his concluding gospel argument in verses 18–20. So

> **How do we glorify God in our bodies? By living a self-consciously gospel-centered life!**

then, *how* do we glorify God in our bodies? By living a self-consciously gospel-centered life! The gospel drives us to flee sexual immorality and to fulfill the chief end of our creation and redemption, which is to glorify God.

Every gospel truth and fruit of the gospel in 1 Corinthians 6:9–20 is aimed directly at the glory of God. The gospel *always* aims at the glory of God first and foremost. That's because in the gospel God's glory shines most fully in the face of Jesus Christ (see 2 Cor. 4:6; John 1:18; Heb. 1:3).

In a sermon titled "Voluntary Suffering," from Isaiah 50:6, John Newton writes,

> Much of the glory of God may be seen, by an enlightened eye, in creation, much in His providential rule and care over His creatures; but the brightness of His glory (John i. 18; Heb. i.

3), the express and full discovery of His perfections, can only be known by Jesus Christ, and the revelation which God has given of Himself to the world by Him.[24]

Through the gospel, the Holy Spirit opens our eyes to receive "the light of the knowledge of the glory of God in the face of Jesus Christ" (2 Cor. 4:6; see 1 Cor. 2:10–14). And, through the gospel, the Holy Spirit creates a desire to glorify God—to enhance His reputation and praise before men (see Matt. 5:16).

This is the essence of regeneration, the creation of a new heart that delights in God and His law (John 14:15; Rom. 7:14–8:4). The heart desire of a gospel-driven believer is to learn what it truly means, as the Westminster Shorter Catechism says, to glorify God and to fully enjoy Him forever.[25] In this context, the call to glorify God in your body means, "Do not give your body to sexual immorality. Do not give yourself to idolatry, which dishonors God and desecrates His holy temple—your body! Rather, live chaste and pure lives whether in marriage or single life" (see 1 Cor. 7:1–9).

If your heart is self-consciously immersed in the gospel realities of being bought by Christ in order to belong to Him and subsequently made into a sacred temple by the indwelling presence of the Holy Spirit, you will be driven to glorify God with your body. As 2 Corinthians 5:14–15 reminds us, "For the love of Christ controls us, because we have concluded this: that one has died for all, therefore all have died; and he died for all, *that those who live might no longer live for themselves but for him who for their sake died and was raised.*"

Before their conversion, the Corinthians had lived for themselves. After their conversion, because they had not grappled with the life implications of the gospel, they insisted on their right to frequent prostitutes. And so, they were living for sexual gratification ("Food is meant for the stomach and the stomach for food"). In contrast, Paul says the gospel-driven believer lives for God and therefore glorifies God.

The distance between Paul and the Corinthians may be measured precisely by the distance between their shallow, self-justifying slogans of 6:12–13, 18 and the bracing command to glorify God with their bodies.[26] A self-conscious gospel focus leads a believer to heed the warning of God's law, flee sexual immorality, and to glorify God in one's body. Paul's gospel-centered arguments maintain that our bodies belong to God and therefore should be used in ways that bring glory, not dishonor, to God.

The gospel doesn't lead us to live for ourselves, to indulge in our selfish, fallen desires of the flesh. No! The gospel of grace drives us to live for God, to follow *His* moral will and interests. The gospel of grace always encourages and drives us to glorify God.

In all this we see that the gospel is not only for *us*. It is also for God's glory! Now that we have been adopted, washed, sanctified, justified, destined for resurrection, united to Christ, indwelt by the Holy Spirit, and bought by Christ to become His purchased possession, we no longer have to live for ourselves—thank God!

These eight gospel truths compel us to glorify God with our bodies, which fulfills the very purpose for which we were created and have been redeemed. Paul's imperatives are the better navigation system, the eight gospel truths are the engine, and the Holy Spirit is the fuel!

REFLECTION

Do you want to flee rather than engage in sexual immorality? Do you want to glorify God with your life? If so, don't try to order it by steps and tips for success. That is a recipe for a shipwreck! As we have said, legal holiness only produces a life that is driven by a series of practices and rules, nourished by checking off items on a list.

Instead, you must go beyond good advice—satellite navigation systems, which rest at the level of our own competence—and instead regularly expose yourself to God's law. A regular diet of law is healthy so long as it is being used lawfully! Question 115 of the Heidelberg Catechism asks, "No one in this life can obey the Ten Commandments perfectly, why then does God want them preached so pointedly?" Here is the answer:

> First, so that the longer we live the more we may come to know our sinfulness and the more eagerly look to Christ for forgiveness of sins and righteousness. Second, so that, while praying to God for the grace of the Holy Spirit, we may never stop striving to be renewed more and more after God's image, until after this life we reach our goal: perfection.[27]

God's law warns us and drives us to Christ and directs us in the path of gratitude.

Second, we must also be constantly nourished in the liberating, purifying, and empowering good news of the gospel of God's grace. We must seek to cultivate a self-conscious knowledge of the gospel and its implications for our lives. This is best done in the context of Christ's visible church where God's people gather weekly to be served Word and Sacrament—the gifts of God for the people of God. By these means of grace the Holy Spirit delivers Christ and all His saving benefits to us week after week, year after year, over a lifetime. Michael Brown and Zach Keele write,

> The Holy Spirit descends to feed our souls through the means he has promised to bless: Christ's preached Word and administered sacraments. By the proclamation of his gospel in the public assembly of his people, God reassures us of his covenant of grace, telling us what our own hearts cannot: that his Son has satisfied the demands of his law in the old covenant and redeemed us from its curse. He kills us with his law, as it were, and raises us up again with his gospel. By the power

of his preached Word, he refreshes our souls with the living water of Christ (John 4:14; 7:37–38), nourishes us so that we may "grow up into salvation" (1 Pet 2:2), and causes our hearts to rejoice in his promise of glorified life (1 Pet 1:8). He also causes us to commune with him by feeding us with the body and blood of Christ in heaven, who secured for us a new and living way into the Holy of Holies. "The cup of blessing that we bless," says Paul, "is it not a participation in the blood of Christ? The bread that we break, is it not a participation in the body of Christ?" (1 Cor. 10:16). When we receive it in faith, as the Heidelberg Catechism says, Christ "himself feeds and nourishes my soul to everlasting life, as certainly as I receive from the hand of the minister and taste with my mouth the bread and cup of the Lord, which are given to me as certain tokens of the body and blood of Christ." Just as the preached gospel is God's new covenant promise, the Lord's Supper is his new covenant meal. Truly, we are assured of his promise and pledge that we are his people and he is our God.[28]

The church's worship is the heart of discipleship.[29] In corporate worship, the Holy Spirit, working through the means of grace, shapes, reforms, and retrains the thoughts and desires of our hearts. He begins making us fit citizens of the kingdom of God. As one writer puts it,

> Discipleship is a kind of immigration, from the kingdom of darkness to the kingdom of God's beloved Son (Col. 1:13). In Christ we are given a heavenly passport; in his body we learn how to live like "locals" of his kingdom. Such an immigra-tion to a new kingdom isn't just a matter of being teleported to a different realm; we need to be acclimated to a new way of life, learn a new language, acquire new habits of that rival dominion. Christian worship is our enculturation as citizens of heaven, subjects of the kingdom to come (Phil. 3:20).[30]

To be sure, discipleship is a life-encompassing, Monday through Saturday included, process that sometimes involves specialized counseling and therapy.[31] But, discipleship "radiates from, and is nourished by, the worship life of the congregation gathered around Word and Table. There is no sanctification without the church, not because some building holds a superstitious magic, but rather because the church is the very body of Christ, animated by the Spirit of God and composed of Spirited practices."[32] Thus, as Timothy Maschke writes,

> Liturgy [the corporate structure of the worship experience and practice] is not something beautiful we do for God, but something beautiful God does for us and among us. Public worship is neither our work nor our possession . . . it is *opus Dei*, God's work. . . liturgy is God's act of blessing His sacred gifts of life and salvation through the ministry of Word and Sacrament and God's people responding to this act of our Divine Liturgist. . . . The liturgy is a vehicle for receiving God's beneficent aid, as well as for our expression of gratitude for His grace. In a sense, the liturgy can be compared to breathing: God's Spirit comes to us (we inhale) and we express our spiritual response back to God (we exhale).[33]

It is not enough to believe that sexual immorality is desecrating, dishonoring, and disastrous—although it certainly is! A God-glorifying life must be driven by the indwelling, life-giving power of the Holy Spirit, as He works through the gospel. We must inhale! The Spirit, working through the ministry of the gospel (both through the audible Word and visible words, namely the sacraments—baptism and the Lord's Supper), will lead you in paths that glorify God (exhale!).

So, let me ask you:

- How often do you dwell on your *adoption*? Do you know that you have been adopted? Adoption—the highest privilege the gospel offers[34]—shows us the meaning and motives of "gospel holiness," which springs from love and gratitude rather than slavish, legal duty. We have been adopted to be holy and blameless (Eph. 1:4–5). God's children love their Father and actively seek to obey His will out of gratitude for such a privileged status. As J. I. Packer writes, "It [gospel holiness] is just a matter of the child of God being true to type, true to His Father, to his Savior and to himself. . . . It is a matter of being a good son or daughter, as distinct from a prodigal or black sheep in the royal family."[35]

- Do you know that you have been *washed*, brought to life by the Holy Spirit? Regeneration is the basis of and power for obedience (see Ezek. 36:25–27). It is not a moral makeover but a whole new identity—a resurrection (Eph. 2:5–6), *ex nihilo* creation (2 Cor. 4:6). Regeneration brings an eternal cleansing, a particular blessing for all who are held captive by regret and shame from sexual failures.

- Do you know that you have been *sanctified*, set apart *by* God *for* God and His holy purposes? Do you therefore know that you are a saint and holy by God's grace?

- Do you know that you have been *justified*, which is the sole basis of your ongoing assurance before God for the times that you have failed (or will fail; see Gal. 5:17; Rom. 7:14–25)? You must be continually reminded that you are righteous before God—even though your conscience accuses you of grievously sinning against all of God's commandments and are still drawn to all evil, like a fly to manure. These charges are true, but God, out of pure grace, imputes to you the perfect satisfaction, righteousness, and the holiness of Christ. He grants these benefits as if you had never committed any sin, and as if you had accomplished all the obedience that Christ has rendered for you.[36]

- Do you know that your body is destined for *resurrection*?
- Do you know that your body is *united to Christ*—that you are a "member of Christ, joined to the Lord"?
- Do you know that your body is a *temple of the Holy Spirit*, a sacred dwelling place purchased by Christ on the cross and thus belonging to Him? This knowledge is exceedingly purifying!
- How central is the corporate worship of the church in the process of your discipleship? Do you regularly avail yourself of the Spirit-empowered means of Word and Sacrament—the gifts of God for the people of God?

As you learn to cultivate a gospel-centered mindset, you will be led by the Holy Spirit increasingly to flee sexual immorality and to glorify God. As you grow in your experiential knowledge of the gospel, you will avoid tempting situations. You will want to heed the warnings of God's law, follow the wisdom of God's law, and delight in obeying the ethical imperatives of God's law.

When you live such a self-consciously gospel-driven life, you will, as one author says, "Display positively in the use of your body the glory and especially the holiness of your heavenly Master who has taken possession of you."[37]

My friend Derek, whom we met in chapter 3, struggled with pornography from the time he was fourteen. He tried numerous programs of Christian asceticism but made no real progress until he encountered the truths of his new identity in Christ, as outlined in 1 Corinthians 6:9–20.

Now Derek, as well as growing numbers of others in my church fellowship, are living out who they are in the Lord—adopted, washed, sanctified, justified, destined for resurrection, united to Christ, indwelt by the Holy Spirit, and bought by Christ to become His purchased possessions. As a consequence, they are learning day by day to glorify God with their bodies.

We're not talking about sinless perfection, but rather a growing joy and power in gratefully obeying the One who accomplished so much for us, leading to more and more freedom from sexual slavery. Such a life is captured in Proverbs 4:18, which says, "But the path of the righteous is like the light of dawn, which shines brighter and brighter until full day."

"I still struggle with lust," Derek says now, "but the power of the gospel and God's love provides more resolve than asceticism ever could."

And the gospel can do the same for you—starting right now.

Soli Deo gloria! Amen.

ACKNOWLEDGMENTS

The origins of this book run deep. It is impossible to thank everyone who has formed my thinking about the gospel and its manifold applications for living out the Christian life. I am especially grateful to Michael Horton, R. Scott Clark, Graeme Goldsworthy, Jerry Bridges, Dennis Johnson, John Stott, Ashley Null, and Dan Cruver. These men have taught me well what it means to be gospel-centered, to see Christ in all the Scriptures, that in our suffering we have a sympathetic Savior, to live in the comforting paradigm of guilt, grace, and gratitude, and to know the adoptive love of the Father in the Son through the Spirit. The impact is eternal. I am forever grateful.

Thanks also to the members of Paramount Church. You have lovingly and faithfully listened to and valued the proclamation of the gospel week after week, year after year. You have learned that faith comes from hearing and hearing by the word of Christ. And you have learned that there is nothing more notable or glorious in the church than the ministry of the gospel. Thanks be to God for His indescribable gift!

A special thanks to Gary Chapman. I took a chance with one of the bestselling authors of our day to read my manuscript and your "love language" response surprised me! You and Karolyn have played a key role in our family over the years. From Karolyn serving as Kathryn's and my wedding coordinator, to your decades of faithful ministry to our family at Calvary, to your books helping us learn how to better love our neighbor, thank you.

A very special thanks is due to Stan Guthrie. When I first preached on 1 Corinthians 6, my initial manuscript that I sent to Stan consisted of lightly edited sermon notes. My seminary training taught me how to write a sermon. Stan taught me how to write a book. He is a gifted and brilliant writer and editor. This book would not exist without Stan. I am grateful for his professional craftmanship as well as his friendship.

I am also grateful for the fine team at Moody Publishers, especially John Hinkley, Pam Pugh, Jacob Iverson, Kathryn Eastham, and Connor Sterchi. Without you, this book and its gospel-centered message of grace and gratitude would never be known or read. Thank you.

I would like to thank my six children—Victoria, Olivia, Wilson, David, Alexandria, and Stuart. You all have patiently and graciously endured Dad's slow, long, winding, gospel-awakening journey. I love you with all my heart.

Finally, to save the best for last, it is a joy to dedicate this volume to my wife, Kathryn. Words escape me. Like Christ, you have seen the worst in me and still love me. You were the first to teach me that the gospel is for Christians. I didn't get this life-transforming truth for the first seven years of our marriage. It took a work of the Spirit and much suffering to teach me what you always knew from the beginning. Thank you for your patience and grace as you have watched me stumble into grace. Your constant love, kindness, wisdom, and gracious spirit sustains and inspires me.

NOTES

Introduction: The Great Disconnect

1. Harriet Sherwood, "Church Sorry for Saying That Sex Is Just for Married Heterosexuals: Church of England Archbishops Acknowledge Pastoral Guidance 'Jeopardised Trust,'" *The Guardian*, January 30, 2020, https://www .theguardian.com/world/2020/jan/30/church-of-england-apologises-over-sex-comments. Western church leaders in the Anglican Communion have continuously sought to undermine Resolution I.10 of the 1998 Lambeth Conference. Resolution I.10 reaffirmed the clear teaching of Scripture on marriage and specifically rejected homosexual practice as incompatible with Scripture. For a detailed account of the decline of the authority of Scripture and the Scripture's clear teaching on marriage within the Anglican Communion, see Stephen Noll, *The Global Anglican Communion: Contending for Anglicanism 1993–2018* (Newport Beach, CA: Anglican House, 2018).

2. Megan Brenan, "Birth Control Still Tops List of Morally Acceptable Issues," Gallup, May 29, 2019, https://news.gallup.com/poll/257858/birth-control-tops-list-morally-acceptable-issues.aspx.

3. Jeff Diamant, "Half of U.S. Christians Say Casual Sex between Consenting Adults Is Sometimes or Always Acceptable," Pew Research Center, August 31, 2020, https://www.pewresearch.org/fact-tank/2020/08/31/half-of-u-s-christians-say-casual-sex-between-consenting-adults-is-sometimes-or-always-acceptable.

4. Morgan Lee, "Here's How 770 Pastors Describe Their Struggle with Porn," *Christianity Today*, January 26, 2016, https://www.christianitytoday.com/news/2016/january/how-pastors-struggle-porn-phenomenon-josh-mcdowell-barna.html.

5. Halee Gray Scott, "Porn Is More Criticized and More Popular Than Ever," *Christianity Today*, June 23, 2016, https://www.christianitytoday.com/ct/2016/julaug/porn-is-simultaneously-more-criticized-and-more-popular-tha.html.

6. Ibid.

7. C. S. Lewis, "We Have No Right to Happiness," *Saturday Evening Post*, April 1, 1982, reposted by Trevin Wax, "C. S. Lewis's Last Written Word: We Have No Right to Happiness," The Gospel Coalition, October 3, 2019, https://www.thegospelcoalition.org/blogs/trevin-wax/c-s-lewis-no-right-happiness/.

8. See "Heidelberg Catechism," in the *Psalter Hymnal: Doctrinal Standards and Liturgy* (Grand Rapids: Board of Publication of the Christian Reformed Church, 1976), 54.

9. Walter Marshall, *The Gospel Mystery of Sanctification: Growing in Holiness by Living in Union with Christ*. Put into modern English by Bruce H. McRae (Eugene, OR: Wipf and Stock, 2005), 7.

10. Ibid.

Chapter 1: Do We Know the Gospel?

1. I am indebted to John Stott for the insights of points 1–3; see John Stott, *Same-Sex Partnerships?: A Christian Perspective* (Grand Rapids: Revell, 1998), 9–13.

2. Michael Horton, *For Calvinism* (Grand Rapids: Zondervan Academic, 2011), 41.

3. Zacharias Ursinus, *The Commentary of Dr. Zacharias Ursinus on the Heidelberg Catechism* (Phillipsburg, NJ: P&R Publishing, 1985), 32. This is a reproduction of the Second American Edition, which was printed at Columbus, Ohio, in 1852.

4. Stott, *Same-Sex Partnerships?*, 9.

5. Michael Horton, *The Christian Faith: A Systematic Theology for Pilgrims on the Way* (Grand Rapids: Zondervan Academic, 2011), 437.

6. Michael Horton, "Covenant," Ligonier Ministries, November 1, 2011, https://www.ligonier.org/learn/articles/covenant.

7. Ibid.

8. Stott, *Same-Sex Partnerships?*, 10.

9. Horton, *For Calvinism*, 36.

10. Ibid., 37.

11. See R. Scott Clark, "Concupiscence: Sin and the Mother of Sin," *The Heidelblog*, January 10, 2015, https://heidelblog.net/2015/01/concupiscence-sin-and-the-mother-of-sin.

12. Horton, *For Calvinism*, 37.

13. Ibid., 41.

14. Stott, *Same-Sex Partnerships?*, 11–12.

15. 1 Corinthians 6:9–11; Galatians 5:19–21; Ephesians 5:3–13; Colossians 3:5–9; 1 Thessalonians 4:1–8.

16. *Heidelberg Catechism, 450th Anniversary Edition* (n.p.: The Synod of the Reformed Church in the U.S., 2013), 64, italics added.

17. See Tim Chester, *Porn-Free Church: Raising Up Gospel Communities to Destroy Secret Sins*, Covenant Eyes, 40, https://www.covenanteyes.com/resources-for-pastors/.

18. John Calvin, *Epistle to the Galatians*, Calvin's Commentaries (Grand Rapids: Baker, 1996), 21:169.
19. Ibid.
20. Ralph Erskine, *The Works of Ralph Erskine*, vol. 2 (Glasgow: Free Presbyterian Publications, 1991), 27.
21. Theodore Beza, *The Christian Faith*, trans. James Clark (East Sussex, UK: Focus Christian Ministries Trust, 1992), 40.
22. 1 Corinthians 6:2–3, 9, 15, 16, 19.
23. Richard B. Hays, *First Corinthians*, Interpretation: A Bible Commentary for Teaching and Preaching (Louisville, KY: Westminster John Knox Press, 2011), 98–103.
24. Craig L. Blomberg, *1 Corinthians*, The NIV Application Commentary (Grand Rapids: Zondervan Academic, 1995), 110.
25. Gordon D. Fee, *The First Epistle to the Corinthians*, The New International Commentary on the New Testament (Grand Rapids: Eerdmans, 1987), 230.
26. Ibid., 251.
27. Graeme Goldsworthy, *According to Plan: The Unfolding Revelation of God in the Bible* (Downers Grove, IL: IVP Academic, 1991), 47, 50.
28. Michael Horton, *Christless Christianity: The Alternative Gospel of the American Church* (Grand Rapids: Baker, 2008), 47.

Chapter 2: Why Do Christians Struggle?

1. See "Heidelberg Catechism," in the *Psalter Hymnal: Doctrinal Standards and Liturgy* (Grand Rapids: Board of Publication of the Christian Reformed Church, 1976), 45.
2. Michael Horton, *God of Promise: Introducing Covenant Theology* (Grand Rapids: Baker, 2006), 193.
3. Ibid., 188.
4. *The Confession of Faith and Catechisms of the Orthodox Presbyterian Church with Proof Texts* (Willow Grove, PA: The Orthodox Presbyterian Church, 2005), 377.
5. Horton, *God of Promise*, 188.
6. Ibid.
7. Michael Horton, *The Christian Faith: A Systematic Theology for Pilgrims on the Way* (Grand Rapids: Zondervan Academic, 2011), 649.
8. Ibid.
9. Mark Galli, *Chaos and Grace: Discovering the Liberating Work of the Holy Spirit* (Grand Rapids: Baker, 2011), 168.
10. David Prior, *The Message of 1 Corinthians*, The Bible Speaks Today: New Testament Series (Downers Grove, IL: IVP Academic, 1985), 87.
11. Jerry Bridges, *Respectable Sins* (Colorado Springs: NavPress, 2017), 14.
12. Horton, *The Christian Faith*, 650.
13. Ibid., 651.
14. Ibid.

15. "Heidelberg Catechism," Christian Reformed Church, accessed May 18, 2022, Q. 62, Q. 114, https://www.crcna.org/welcome/beliefs/confessions/heidelberg-catechism.

16. Book of Common Prayer, 1662 edition.

17. For a brief explanation of this important theological concept, see Daniel Dunlap, "Living in the Tension," Ligonier Ministries, May 1, 1992, https://www.ligonier.org/learn/articles/living-in-the-tension/.

18. Horton, *The Christian Faith*, 658.

19. Ibid., 660.

20. Vaughan Roberts, *God's Big Picture: Tracing the Storyline of the Bible* (Downers Grove, IL: IVP Books, 2002), 133.

21. J. I. Packer, *Keep in Step with the Spirit* (Grand Rapids: Revell, 1984), 157.

22. Michael Horton gives this important qualification when it comes to the believer's progress in holiness: "We should beware of turning the distinction into a separation, where our status as holy in Christ is one thing and our own progress in holiness is another. In our pilgrimage, we are not simply growing in *our* holiness, but bearing the fruit of our union with Christ and *his* holiness. The flesh (*sarx*) is not given a new lease on life, improved, elevated, and revived. Rather, the Adamic self is put to death, and the person thus raised is now a participant in the Spirit, sharing with Christ in the powers of the age to come. Thus, our justification and union with Christ cannot be seen merely as the starting point for a life of personal transformation, but as the only source of any fecundity throughout the Christian life. Our mortification and vivification in sanctification are not our own contribution alongside justification and union with Christ, but are the effect of that new relationship. Nevertheless, it is not Christ who dies and rises daily, putting to death indwelling sins, but believers. Faith is given in regeneration and passively receives justification, but in sanctification it is active in love." *The Christian Faith*, 653.

23. Ibid., 653.

24. Ibid., 652.

25. Ibid., 653.

Chapter 3: Who Can't Inherit the Kingdom?

1. Gordon D. Fee, *The First Epistle to the Corinthians,* The New International Commentary on the New Testament (Grand Rapids: Eerdmans, 1987), 250.

2. Irving L. Jensen, *Jensen's Survey of the New Testament* (Chicago: Moody, 1981), 265.

3. David Prior, *The Message of 1 Corinthians,* The Bible Speaks Today: New Testament Series (Downers Grove, IL: IVP Academic, 1985), 70.

4. Fee, *The First Epistle to the Corinthians*, 3.

5. Ibid., 196–97.

6. Simon J. Kistemaker, *1 Corinthians*, New Testament Commentary Series (Grand Rapids: Baker, 1993), 187.

7. Charles Hodge, *Commentary on the First Epistle to the Corinthians* (Grand Rapids: Eerdmans, 1980), 98.

8. See Graeme Goldsworthy, *Gospel and Kingdom* (Milton Keynes, UK: Paternoster, 2000), 46; and Vaughan Roberts, *God's Big Picture: Tracing the Storyline of the Bible* (Downers Grove, IL: IVP Books, 2002), 21.

9. Roberts, *God's Big Picture*, 21.

10. Ibid., 123–35.

11. Graeme Goldsworthy, *Preaching the Whole Bible as Christian Scripture: The Application of Biblical Theology to Expository Preaching* (Grand Rapids: Eerdmans, 2000), 55.

12. Samuel Bolton, *The True Bounds of Christian Freedom* (Carlisle, PA: The Banner of Truth Trust, 1965), 72.

13. Prior, *The Message of 1 Corinthians*, 91.

14. See Robert Gagnon, *The Bible and Homosexual Practice: Texts and Hermeneutics* (Nashville: Abingdon Press, 2001), 305.

15. "Heidelberg Catechism," Christian Reformed Church, accessed May 18, 2022, Q. 94–95, https://www.crcna.org/welcome/beliefs/confessions/heidelberg-catechism.

16. Fee, *The First Epistle to the Corinthians*, 243.

17. David E. Garland, *1 Corinthians*, Baker Exegetical Commentary on the New Testament (Grand Rapids: Baker Academic, 2003), 235–36.

18. Gagnon, *The Bible and Homosexual Practice*, 306.

19. Ibid., 313, n99.

20. Ibid., 306.

21. Ibid., 312.

22. Ibid., 306.

23. On January 19, 2021, the Anglican Church in North America College of Bishops issued a Pastoral Statement titled "Sexuality and Identity: A Pastoral Statement from the College of Bishops." The statement advised against using the designation "gay Christian." The statement in part reads, "To insist on the adjective 'gay,' with all of its cultural attachments, is problematic to the point that we cannot affirm its usage in relation to the word 'Christian,'" https://anglicanchurch.net/sexuality-and-identity-a-pastoral-statement-from-the-college-of-bishops/.

24. Garland, *1 Corinthians*, 215.

25. Ibid.

26. See "Canons of Dort," in the *Psalter Hymnal, Doctrinal Standards and Liturgy* (Grand Rapids: Board of Publications of the Christian Reformed Church, 1976), Article 1, 109.

27. Samuel L. Bray and Drew Nathaniel Keane, eds., *The Book of Common Prayer and Administration of the Sacraments and Other Rites and Ceremonies of the Church*, International Edition (Downers Grove, IL: IVP Academic, 2021), 631.

28. John Owen, *The Works of John Owen*, ed. William H. Goold (Edinburgh: The Banner of Truth Trust, 2005), 6:12.

29. Prior, *The Message of 1 Corinthians*, 88–89.

30. Geoffrey B. Wilson, *Galatians*, New Testament Commentaries (Edinburgh: The Banner of Truth Trust, 1979), 251.

Chapter 4: Who Can Inherit the Kingdom?

1. John Calvin, *Calvin's Commentaries on the Epistles of Paul the Apostle to the Corinthians*, ed. John Pringle (Grand Rapids: Baker, 1996), I:211.

2. I am indebted to Graeme Goldsworthy for this idea of Jesus exercising His kingly power through the scepter of His preached gospel. See Graeme Goldsworthy, *Preaching the Whole Bible as Christian Scripture* (Grand Rapids: Eerdmans, 2000), 55.

3. See "Canons of Dort," in the *Psalter Hymnal, Doctrinal Standards and Liturgy* (Grand Rapids: Board of Publications of the Christian Reformed Church, 1976), Article 17; see 1 Peter 1:23.

4. John Murray, *Redemption Accomplished and Applied* (Grand Rapids: Eerdmans, 1955), 96.

5. Craig Blomberg, *1 Corinthians*, The NIV Application Commentary (Grand Rapids: Zondervan Academic, 1995), 209–10.

6. Murray, *Redemption Accomplished and Applied*, 100.

7. Michael Horton, *The Christian Faith: A Systematic Theology for Pilgrims on the Way* (Grand Rapids: Zondervan Academic, 2011), 1000.

8. Blomberg, *1 Corinthians*, 215.

9. See the encounter in John 3.

10. Philip Graham Ryken, Derek W. H. Thomas, and J. Ligon Duncan III, eds., *Give Praise to God: A Vision for Reforming Worship* (Phillipsburg, NJ: P&R Publishing, 2003), 171.

11. Ed Welch, *When People Are Big and God Is Small: Overcoming Peer Pressure, Codependency, and the Fear of Man* (Phillipsburg, NJ: P&R Publishing, 1997), 25.

12. Ibid., 26–27.

13. "Heidelberg Catechism," *Psalter Hymnal*, 35.

14. *The Confession of Faith and Catechisms of The Orthodox Presbyterian Church with Proof Texts*, reprint ed. (Willow Grove, PA: The Orthodox Presbyterian Church, 2008), 377. Published by and available from: The Committee on Christian Education of the Orthodox Presbyterian Church, 607 N. Easton Road, Bldg. E. Box P., Willow Grove, PA, 19090-0920.

15. Charles A. Wanamaker, *The Epistles to the Thessalonians: A Commentary on the Greek Text*, New International Greek Testament Commentary (Grand Rapids: Eerdmans, 1990), 157.

16. Ewald M. Plass, *What Luther Says* (St. Louis, MO: Concordia Publishing House, 1959), 704.

17. *Heidelberg Catechism, 450th Anniversary Edition* (n.p.: The Synod of the Reformed Church in the United States, 2013), 64.

18. Jerry Bridges, *The Gospel for Real Life: Turn to the Liberating Power of the Cross . . . Every Day* (Colorado Springs: NavPress, 2003), 178.

19. For more on the double benefit of Christ, see R. Scott Clark, *Caspar Olevian and the Substance of the Covenant: The Double Benefit of Christ* (Edinburgh: Rutherford House, 2005).

20. John Calvin, *Commentary on the Epistles of Paul the Apostle to the Corinthians* (Grand Rapids: Baker, 1996), 93.

21. John Calvin, *Institutes of the Christian Religion,* ed. John T. McNeill, trans. Ford Lewis Battles, The Library of Christian Classics (Philadelphia: The Westminster Press, 1960), 20:798.

22. Walter Marshall, *The Gospel Mystery of Sanctification: Growing in Holiness by Living in Union with Christ.* Put into modern English by Bruce H. McRae (Eugene, OR: Wipf and Stock, 2005), 115.

23. Ibid., 116.

24. Ibid.

25. Anglican Church in North America, *The Book of Common Prayer* (Huntington Beach, CA: Anglican Liturgy Press, 2019), 776–77.

26. William Perkins, ed. Paul M. Smalley, Joel R. Beeke, and Derek W. H. Thomas, *The Works of William Perkins* (Grand Rapids: Reformation Heritage Books, 2015), 2:162.

27. Bridges, *The Gospel for Real Life,* 110.

28. Marshall, *The Gospel Mystery of Sanctification,* 125.

29. Ibid., 139.

30. Michael Horton, "The God-Centered Gospel," Ligonier Ministries, April 1, 2012, http://www.ligonier.org/learn/articles/god-centered-gospel.

31. Ibid.

32. Blomberg, *1 Corinthians,* 212.

33. Calvin, *Institutes of the Christian Religion,* 3.1.1.

34. J. I. Packer, *Knowing God* (Downers Grove, IL: InterVarsity Press, 2021), 223.

35. Blomberg, *1 Corinthians,* 215.

36. "Heidelberg Catechism," *Psalter Hymnal,* 32.

37. Gordon D. Fee, *The First Epistle to the Corinthians,* The New International Commentary on the New Testament (Grand Rapids: Eerdmans, 1987), 248.

Chapter 5: Our Bodies Will Live Forever

1. For an excellent summary of the slogans used by the Corinthians, see Denny Burk, "Discerning Corinthian Slogans through Paul's Use of the Diatribe in 1 Corinthians 6:12–20," *Bulletin for Biblical Research* 18, no. 1 (2008): 99–121.

2. Gordon D. Fee, *The First Epistle to the Corinthians,* The New International Commentary on the New Testament (Grand Rapids: Eerdmans, 1987), 250.

3. The slogans represent real voices within the Corinthian church; see Burk, "Discerning Corinthian Slogans in 1 Cor 6:12–20," 110.

4. Fee, *The First Epistle to the Corinthians,* 253.

5. See Anthony C. Thiselton, *1 Corinthians: A Shorter Exegetical and Pastoral Commentary* (Grand Rapids: Eerdmans, 2011), 461; Richard B. Hays, *First Corinthians*, Interpretation: A Bible Commentary for Teaching and Preaching (Louisville, KY: Westminster John Knox Press, 2011), 101.

6. Walter Bauer and Frederick William Danker, *A Greek-English Lexicon of the New Testament and Other Early Christian Literature*, 3rd ed. (Chicago: University of Chicago Press, 2001), 960.

7. Fee, *The First Epistle to the Corinthians*, 252.

8. See 1 Corinthians 9:1, 9; see also Hays, *First Corinthians*, 101.

9. Samuel Bolton, *The True Bounds of Christian Freedom* (Carlisle, PA: The Banner of Truth Trust, 1965), 72.

10. Burk, "Discerning Corinthian Slogans in 1 Cor 6:12–20," 114, n32.

11. "Heidelberg Catechism," *Psalter Hymnal*, 8.

12. Thiselton, *The First Epistle to the Corinthians*, 1186.

13. Graeme Goldsworthy, *Preaching the Whole Bible as Christian Scripture* (Grand Rapids: Eerdmans, 2000), 57, 59.

14. Ben Witherington, *Conflict & Community in Corinth* (Grand Rapids: Eerdmans, 1995), 164, n11.

15. Hays, *First Corinthians*, 104.

16. Fee, *The First Epistle to the Corinthians*, 256–57.

17. Ibid., 257.

18. *Psalter Hymnal*, 3.

19. Ibid., 28.

20. David E. Garland, *1 Corinthians*, Baker Exegetical Commentary on the New Testament (Grand Rapids: Baker Academic, 2003), 232.

21. Fee, *The First Epistle to the Corinthians*, 257.

22. Ibid., 251.

23. J. I. Packer and Gary A. Parrett, *Grounded in the Gospel: Building Believers the Old-Fashioned Way* (Grand Rapids: Baker, 2010), 118–21.

Chapter 6: Our Bodies Are United with Christ

1. John Calvin, *Commentary on the Epistles of Paul the Apostle to the Corinthians* (Grand Rapids: Baker, 1996), I:216.

2. John Murray, *Redemption Accomplished and Applied* (Grand Rapids: Eerdmans, 1955), 161.

3. Ibid.

4. Gordon D. Fee, *The First Epistle to the Corinthians*, The New International Commentary on the New Testament (Grand Rapids: Eerdmans, 1987), 250.

5. Kenneth Schenck, *1 & 2 Corinthians: A Commentary for Bible Students* (Indianapolis: Wesleyan Publishing House, 2006), 97.

6. Richard B. Hays, *First Corinthians*, Interpretation: A Bible Commentary for Teaching and Preaching (Louisville, KY: Westminster John Knox Press, 2011), 102.

7. John Calvin, *Calvin's Commentaries on the Epistles of Paul the Apostle to the Corinthians*, I:213.

8. "Heidelberg Catechism," *Psalter Hymnal*, 8.

9. John Calvin, *Institutes of the Christian Religion*, ed. John T. McNeill, trans. Ford Lewis Battles, The Library of Christian Classics (Philadelphia: The Westminster Press, 1960), 3.1.1.

10. Jerry Bridges, *The Gospel for Real Life: Turn to the Liberating Power of the Cross . . . Every Day* (Colorado Springs: NavPress, 2003), 39.

11. Fee, *The First Epistle to the Corinthians*, 258.

12. Ibid.

13. David E. Garland, *1 Corinthians*, Baker Exegetical Commentary on the New Testament (Grand Rapids: Baker Academic, 2003), 234.

14. Craig Blomberg, *1 Corinthians*, The NIV Application Commentary (Grand Rapids: Zondervan Academic, 1995), 218.

15. The Septuagint, abbreviated LXX, consists of the Old Testament and Apocrypha translated into Koine Greek in the centuries before Christ and adopted by the apostles and the early church.

16. Alfred Rahlfs, ed., *Septuaginta, Accordance Bible Software* (Stuttgart: Deutsche Bibelgesellschaft, 2006).

17. Ibid.

18. Commenting on the covenant of grace, Michael Brown and Zach Keele write, "The essence of the covenant of grace is summarized in God's promise: 'I will be your God, and you shall be my people.' This promise echoes throughout redemptive history. God made this promise to Abraham when he ordained the covenant sign of circumcision (Gen. 17:7). Over four hundred years later, God made this same promise to Abraham's biological descendants when he brought them out of slavery in Egypt (Ex. 6:7). He made it to them again as he prescribed the blessings they would inherit for their obedience to the Sinai covenant (Lev. 26:11–12). Much later in Israel's history, after centuries of disobedience to the Sinai covenant, God made this promise again, this time in connection to his promise of a new covenant (Jer. 31:33; see Ezek. 34:23–24; 37:26–27). This same promise is also found in the New Testament as Paul applies it to believers, both Jew and Gentile (2 Cor. 6:16). Finally, we hear this promise in the closing chapters of Revelation, which record John's vision of a new heaven and new earth in the future (Rev. 21:2–3). Thus, God's promise in the one covenant of grace runs from Genesis to Revelation, revealing its continuity and the unifying nature of redemptive history." *Sacred Bond: Covenant Theology Explored Second Edition* (Grandville, MI: Reformed Fellowship, Inc., 2012), 66.

19. "You shall not commit adultery" (Ex. 20:14). For interesting and concise comments on this commandment, see "The Seventh Commandment," Ligonier Ministries, September 6, 2010.

20. Dennis E. Johnson, *Him We Proclaim: Preaching Christ from All the Scripture* (Phillipsburg, NJ: P&R Publishing, 2007), 54.

21. Blomberg, *1 Corinthians*, 216.
22. Calvin, *Calvin's Commentaries on the Epistles of Paul the Apostle to the Corinthians*, 216.
23. *Heidelberg Catechism, 450th Anniversary Edition* (The Synod of the Reformed Church in the United States, 2013).

Chapter 7: Our Bodies Are Temples of the Holy Spirit

1. *ESV Study Bible* (Wheaton, IL: Crossway Bibles, 2008), 2189.
2. Encyclopedia Britannica editors, "Aphrodite," Encyclopedia Britannica, updated September 24, 2020, https://www.britannica.com/topic/Aphrodite-Greek-mythology.
3. Everett Ferguson writes, "Both Jewish and Christian writers agreed that the Greco-Roman world was characterized by moral corruption. The Jewish apologists said that the low morality sprang from idolatry." *Backgrounds of Early Christianity* (Grand Rapids: Eerdmans, 2003), 70. See also *ESV Study Bible*, 2189.
4. D. A. Carson and Douglas J. Moo, *An Introduction to the New Testament* (Grand Rapids: Zondervan, 2005), 427.
5. Ibid., 427.
6. Gordon D. Fee, *The First Epistle to the Corinthians*, The New International Commentary on the New Testament (Grand Rapids: Eerdmans, 1987), 250.
7. Ibid., 147.
8. "When you are assembled in the name of the Lord Jesus and my spirit is present, with the power of our Lord Jesus, you are to deliver this man to Satan for the destruction of the flesh, so that his spirit may be saved in the day of the Lord" (1 Cor. 5:4–5).
9. Michael Brown and Zach Keele, *Sacred Bond: Covenant Theology Explored* (Grandville, MI: Reformed Fellowship, Inc., 2012), 66.
10. Ibid., 66.
11. Ibid.
12. Ibid.
13. Fee, *The First Epistle to the Corinthians*, 148.
14. Daniel Hyde, *God in Our Midst: The Tabernacle and Our Relationship with God* (Sanford, FL: Reformation Trust Publishing, 2012), 20.
15. Ibid., 3.
16. Ibid., 23.
17. Ibid., 26–27.
18. See Hebrews 8:5.
19. Biblical Studies Press, *The NET Bible with Strong's, Second Edition* Electronic text hypertexted and prepared by OakTree Software, Inc. Version 4.5 (Nashville: Thomas Nelson, 2019), 1 Cor. 6:18–20.
20. Denny Burk, "Discerning Corinthian Slogans through Paul's Use of the Diatribe in 1 Corinthians 6:12–20," *Bulletin for Biblical Research* 18, no. 1 (2008): 117–18.

21. Concerning 1 Corinthians 6:18, the NET writes, "It is debated whether this is a Corinthian slogan. If it is not, then Paul is essentially arguing that there are two types of sin, nonsexual sins which take place outside the body and sexual sins which are against a person's very own body. If it is a Corinthian slogan, then it is a slogan used by the Corinthians to justify their immoral behavior. With it they are claiming that anything done in the body or through the body had no moral relevance. A decision here is very difficult, but the latter is to be preferred for two main reasons. (1) This is the most natural understanding of the statement as it is written. To construe it as a statement by Paul requires a substantial clarification in the sense (e.g., "All *other* sins . . ." [NIV]). (2) Theologically the former is more difficult: Why would Paul single out sexual sins as more intrinsically related to the body than other sins, such as gluttony or drunkenness? For these reasons, it is more likely that the phrase in quotation marks is indeed a Corinthian slogan which Paul turns against them in the course of his argument, although the decision must be regarded as tentative." *The NET Bible with Strong's, Second Edition* (Nashville: Thomas Nelson, 2019), 1 Cor. 6:18.

22. Richard B. Hays, *First Corinthians: Interpretation: A Bible Commentary for Teaching and Preaching* (Louisville, KY: Westminster John Knox Press, 2011), 105.

23. *A Greek-English Lexicon of the New Testament and Other Early Christian Literature,* 3rd ed. *(BDAG)* (Chicago: University of Chicago Press, 2000), 1052.

24. Paul issues the same exhortation in 10:14 regarding idolatry, perhaps because of the close connection between sexual immorality and idolatry in Israel's history (see Ex. 34:15–16; Num. 25:1–3; Ezek. 23; Hos. 4:12–15).

25. Augustine of Hippo, "On the Trinity," in *Augustine: On the Holy Trinity, Doctrinal Treatises, Moral Treatises,* ed. Philip Schaff (Peabody, MA: Hendrickson Publishers, 2004), 3:219.

26. See Jordan Stone, *A Communion of Love: The Christ-Centered Spirituality of Robert Murray M'Cheyne* (Eugene, OR: Wipf and Stock, 2019), 91.

27. Calvin's *Commentaries,* vol. 20, 220.

28. For the descriptive phrase "God's empowering presence," I am indebted to Gordon D. Fee, *God's Empowering Presence: The Holy Spirit in the Letters of Paul* (Peabody, MA: Hendrickson Publishers, 1994).

29. *Christian Creeds and Confessions* (Christ Reformed Church, 2011), 35.

30. Q. 114 in the Heidelberg Catechism states, "But can those who are converted to God obey these commandments perfectly? No. In this life even the holiest have only a small beginning of this obedience. Nevertheless, with all seriousness of purpose, they do begin to live according to all, not only some, of God's commandments," See "Heidelberg Catechism," in *Psalter Hymnal, Doctrinal Standards and Liturgy,* 56.

31. *The Confession of Faith and Catechisms of the Orthodox Presbyterian Church with Proof Texts* (Willow Grove, PA: The Orthodox Presbyterian Church, 2005), 377.

32. See Jerry Bridges, *The Discipline of Grace: God's Role and Our Role in the Pursuit of Holiness* (Colorado Springs: NavPress, 1994), 94.

33. Robert Murray M'Cheyne, *A Basket of Fragments: Notes for Revival* (Scotland, UK: Christian Focus Publications, 1996), 286.

34. Paul Barnett, *1 Corinthians: Holiness and Hope of a Rescued People*, Focus on the Bible Commentary (Scotland, UK: Christian Focus Publications, 2000), 104.

35. In Romans 5:5 Paul writes, "God's love has been poured into our hearts through the Holy Spirit who has been given to us."

36. Barnett, *1 Corinthians*, 103.

37. Robert Murray M'Cheyne, "The Love of Christ," https://www.the-highway.com/articleAug11.html.

38. Walter Marshall, *The Gospel Mystery of Sanctification: Growing in Holiness by Living in Union with Christ.* Put into modern English by Bruce H. McRae (Eugene, OR: Wipf and Stock, 2005), 236.

39. See 1 Corinthians 6:9–10; see Calvin, *Institutes*, 3.2.12.

40. See "Heidelberg Catechism," in *Psalter Hymnal, Doctrinal Standards and Liturgy* (Grand Rapids: Board of Publication of the Christian Reformed Church, 1976), 56.

41. Calvin, *Institutes*, 4.1.5.

42. "Heidelberg Catechism," *Psalter Hymnal*, 56.

43. Marshall, *The Gospel Mystery of Sanctification*, 31.

Chapter 8: Our Bodies Were Bought by Christ on the Cross

1. *The Confession of Faith and Catechisms of the Orthodox Presbyterian Church with Proof Texts* (Willow Grove, PA: The Orthodox Presbyterian Church, 2005), 377.

2. J. I. Packer and Gary A. Parrett, *Grounded in the Gospel: Building Believers the Old-Fashioned Way* (Grand Rapids: Baker Books, 2010), 109.

3. David E. Garland, *1 Corinthians*, Baker Exegetical Commentary on the New Testament (Grand Rapids: Baker Academic, 2003), 239.

4. See Tony Perrottet, "Ancient Greek Temples of Sex," November 21, 2007, https://www.thesmartset.com/article11210701/.

5. "The Roman institution of being a 'bondservant' or 'slave' (Gk. *Doulos* . . .) was different from the institution of slavery in North America during the seventeenth through the nineteenth centuries. Slaves (bondservants, servants) generally were permitted to work for pay and to save enough to buy their freedom (see Matt. 25:15 where the 'servants' [again Gk. *doulos*] were entrusted with immense amounts of money and responsibility). The NT assumes that trafficking in human beings is a sin (1 Tim. 1:10; Rev. 18:11–13), and Paul urges Christian bondservants who can gain . . . freedom to do so. The released bondservant was officially designated a 'freedman' and frequently continued to work for his former master. Many extant inscriptions from freedmen indicate the tendency to adopt the family name of their former master (now their 'patron') and to continue honoring them." *ESV Study Bible* (Wheaton, IL: Crossway Bibles, 2008), 2201.

6. *A Greek-English Lexicon of the New Testament and Other Early Christian Literature*, 3rd ed. *(BDAG)* (Chicago: University of Chicago Press, 2000), 14.

7. Garland, *1 Corinthians*, 239.

8. See, for example, Colossians 2:15.

9. Jerry Bridges, *The Gospel for Real Life: Turn to the Liberating Power of the Cross . . . Every Day* (Colorado Springs: NavPress, 2003), 81.

10. Leon Morris, *The Cross in the New Testament* (Grand Rapids: Eerdmans, 1965), 322.

11. David Prior, *The Message of 1 Corinthians*: The Bible Speaks Today: New Testament Series (Downers Grove, IL: IVP Academic, 1985), 103.

12. Bridges, *The Gospel for Real Life*, 81.

13. Garland, *1 Corinthians*, 239.

14. Ibid.

15. *ESV Study Bible*, Hosea 3:1, 1626.

16. Garland, *1 Corinthians*, 239.

17. Michael G. Brown and Zach Keele, *Sacred Bond: Covenant Theology Explored* (Grandville, MI: Reformed Fellowship, Inc., 2012), 66.

18. Ibid., 66.

19. Christopher Wright, *The Mission of God: Unlocking the Bible's Grand Narrative* (Downers Grove, IL: InterVarsity Press, 2006), 265.

20. See also Exodus 34:9 where Moses prays, "If now I have found favor in your sight, O Lord, please let the Lord go in the midst of us, for it is a stiff-necked people, and pardon our iniquity and our sin, *and take us for your inheritance.*" Moses knows that God's people, who are east of Eden, banished from the presence of God, need Him to dwell in their midst or it is pointless for Israel to continue. In Deuteronomy 7:6, Moses says to the people, "For you are a people holy to the LORD your God. The LORD your God has chosen you to be a people *for His treasured possession*, out of all the peoples who are on the face of the earth" (see Deut. 14:2; 26:18). To be holy to the Lord is to be set apart exclusively to God; to belong to Him (see 6:11, "sanctified"). In 1 Samuel 12:22, Samuel reminds God's people, "For the LORD will not forsake His people, for His great name's sake, because it has pleased the LORD *to make you a people for Himself.*" God promises to not deal with His chosen people according to their sin but rather to treat them mercifully "for His great name's sake." This is grace—divine favor! We belong to God by grace to the praise of His glory (i.e., the covenant relation with God is possible because of His steadfast love, which is for His name's sake; see Eph. 1:3–14).

21. Edmund Clowney, *Preaching Christ in All of Scripture* (Wheaton, IL: Crossway, 2003), 53.

22. Concerning *sola fide*, Q. 64 in the Heidelberg Catechism asks, "But doesn't this teaching make men careless and wicked?" Here's the answer, "No, for it is impossible that those who are grafted into Christ by true faith should not bring forth fruits of thankfulness. Mt 7:18; Lk 6:43–45; Jn 15:5." See "Heidelberg

Catechism", in *Psalter Hymnal: Doctrinal Standards and Liturgy* (Grand Rapids: Board of Publication of the Christian Reformed Church, 1976), 31.

23. See Ashley Null, *Divine Allurement: Cranmer's Comfortable Words* (London: The Latimer Trust, 2014), 3–5.

24. Ibid., 4.

25. Ibid., 4–5.

Chapter 9: The Goal of Sexual Purity

1. *The Confession of Faith and Catechisms of the Orthodox Presbyterian Church with Proof Texts* (Willow Grove, PA: The Orthodox Presbyterian Church, 2005), 355.

2. Thomas Watson, *A Body of Divinity* (Carlisle, PA: The Banner of Truth Trust, 1992), 6.

3. Ibid., 6; see John 12:41; 17:5, 24.

4. Ibid., 7.

5. *A Greek-English Lexicon of the New Testament and Other Early Christian Literature,* 3rd ed. *(BDAG)* (Chicago: University of Chicago Press, 2000), 258.

6. J. I. Packer, *Knowing God* (Downers Grove, IL: InterVarsity Press, 1973), 200.

7. Michael Horton, *God of Promise: Introducing Covenant Theology* (Grand Rapids: Baker, 2006), 193.

8. Graeme Goldsworthy, *Preaching the Whole Bible as Christian Scripture* (Grand Rapids: Eerdmans, 2000), xiv.

9. Ibid., 118.

10. Ibid., 115.

11. Horton, *God of Promise*, 188.

12. I am indebted to Michael Horton for this illustration. See Horton, *God of Promise*, 193–94.

13. See "The Westminster Larger Catechism," Q. 155, http://www.freepresbyterian .org/uploads/Larger_Catechism.pdf.

14. For a helpful series on the errors of nomism and antinomianism, see "Heidelcast Series: Nomism and Antinomianism," August 29, 2018, https://heidelblog .net/2018/08/heidelcast-series-nomism-and-antinomianism.

15. J. I. Packer, *Knowing God* (Downers Grove, IL: InterVarsity Press, 2021), 200.

16. Ibid. Regarding the term "Puritan," R. Scott Clark writes, "the very designation 'the Puritans' is a better marketing catchphrase than historical denominator. . . . A volume titled *A Variety of English Pastors with Varying Sympathies with the Reformation and United by Similar Method and Passion for Holiness* would not be nearly as marketable as a volume on 'The Puritans' but it would be more accurate." See R. Scott Clark, "Review of J. I. Packer, Puritan Portraits," *The Heidelblog*, November 24, 2015, https://heidelblog.net/2015/11/ review-of-j-i-packer-puritan-portraits.

17. Michael Horton, *The Christian Faith: A Systematic Theology for Pilgrims on the Way* (Grand Rapids: Zondervan Academic, 2011), 717.

18. Graeme Goldsworthy, *Preaching the Whole Bible as Christian Scripture* (Grand Rapids: Eerdmans, 2000), xiv.

19. Horton, *God of Promise*, 191.

20. "Heidelberg Catechism," *Psalter Hymnal*, 8.

21. Note: There are two "flee" statements in the letter: one having to do with idolatry (ch. 10), the other sexual immorality (ch. 6). These were typically Paul's two main warnings when dealing with Gentile converts. Paul always ties these two sins together; see Galatians 5:19–21.

22. Gordon D. Fee, *The First Epistle to the Corinthians*, The New International Commentary on the New Testament (Grand Rapids: Eerdmans, 1987), 263.

23. John Murray, *Redemption Accomplished and Applied* (Grand Rapids: Eerdmans, 1955), 161.

24. John Newton, "Sermon XVIII," in *The Works of John Newton*, vol. 4 (Carlisle, PA: The Banner of Truth Trust, 1988), 212–13.

25. Romans 7:14–25; 11:36; 1 Corinthians 10:31; Psalm 16; 73:24, 28; John 17:21–23.

26. Richard B. Hays, *First Corinthians: Interpretation: A Bible Commentary for Teaching and Preaching* (Louisville, KY: Westminster John Knox Press, 2011), 106.

27. *Psalter Hymnal*, 56.

28. Michael G. Brown and Zach Keele, *Sacred Bond: Covenant Theology Explored* (Grandville, MI: Reformed Fellowship, Inc., 2012), 148–49.

29. James K. A. Smith, *You Are What You Love: The Spiritual Power of Habit* (Grand Rapids: Brazos Press, 2016), 68.

30. Ibid., 66.

31. Ibid., 68.

32. Ibid.

33. Timothy H. Maschke, *Gathered Guests: A Guide to Worship in the Lutheran Church*, 2nd ed. (St. Louis, MO: Concordia Publishing House, 2009), 125. "Liturgy is not something beautiful we do for God, but something beautiful God does for us and among us. Public worship is neither our work nor our possession . . . it is *opus Dei*, God's work" is often quoted and is from Nathan D. Mitchell, "The Amen Corner: 'Being Good and Being Beautiful,'" *Worship* 74, no. 6 (November 2000): xvi.

34. Packer, *Knowing God*, 187.

35. Ibid., 186.

36. "Heidelberg Catechism," *Psalter Hymnal*, 30.

37. Frederic Louis Godet, *Commentary on First Corinthians*, vol. 1 (Grand Rapids: Kregel Publications, 1985), 314.

BIBLIOGRAPHY

Arndt, William, et al. *A Greek-English Lexicon of the New Testament and Other Early Christian Literature.* Chicago: University of Chicago Press, 2000.

Barclay, William. *The Letters to the Corinthians Revised Edition.* The Daily Study Bible Series. Philadelphia: The Westminster Press, 1975.

Barnett, Paul. *1 Corinthians: Holiness and Hope of a Rescued People.* Focus on the Bible Commentary. Scotland, UK: Christian Focus Publications, 2000.

Bauer, Walter, and Frederick William Danker. *A Greek-English Lexicon of the New Testament and Other Early Christian Literature,* 3rd Edition. Chicago: University of Chicago Press, 2001.

Baugh, S. M. "Cult Prostitution in New Testament Ephesus: A Reappraisal." JETS 42/3 (September 1999): 443–60. https://www.etsjets.org/files/JETS-PDFs/42/42-3/42-3-pp443-460_JETS.pdf.

Beza, Theodore. *The Christian Faith,* trans. James Clark. East Sussex: Focus Christian Ministries Trust, 1992.

Biblical Studies Press. *The NET Bible with Strong's, Second Edition.* Electronic text hypertexted and prepared by OakTree Software, Inc. Version 4.5. Nashville: Thomas Nelson, 2019.

Blomberg, Craig. *1 Corinthians*. The NIV Application Commentary. Grand Rapids: Zondervan Publishing House, 1994.

Bolton, Samuel. *The True Bounds of Christian Freedom*. Carlisle, PA: The Banner of Truth Trust, 1965.

Bridges, Jerry. *The Gospel for Real Life: Turning to the Liberating Power of the Cross . . . Every Day*. Colorado Springs: NavPress, 2003.

———. *Respectable Sins: Confronting the Sins We Tolerate*. Colorado Springs: NavPress, 2007.

———. *The Discipline of Grace: God's Role and Our Role in the Pursuit of Holiness*. NavPress, 1994.

Brown, Michael and Zach Keele. *Sacred Bond: Covenant Theology Explored*. Grandville: Reformed Fellowship, Inc. 2012.

Burk, Denny. "Discerning Corinthian Slogans through Paul's Use of the Diatribe in 1 Corinthians 6:12–20," *Bulletin for Biblical Research* 18, no. 1 (2008): 99–121.

Calvin: Institutes of the Christian Religion. Edited by John T. McNeill. Translated by Ford Lewis Battles. Vols. 20 and 21 of *The Library of Christian Classics*. Philadelphia: Westminster Press, 1960.

Calvin, John. *Calvin's Commentaries*. Vols. 20, 21. Grand Rapids: Baker Book House, 1996.

Cambridge University. *1662 Book of Common Prayer, Enlarged Edition*. Cambridge University Press, 2006.

Carson, D. A. and Douglas J. Moo. *An Introduction to the New Testament*. Grand Rapids: Zondervan, 2005.

Chester, Tim. *Porn-Free Church: Raising Up Gospel Communities to Destroy Secret Sins*, Covenant Eyes, https://www.covenanteyes.com/resources-for-pastors/.

Christ Reformed Church. *Christian Creeds and Confessions.* 2011.

Clark, R. Scott. *Caspar Olevian and the Substance of the Covenant: The Double Benefit of Christ.* Edinburgh: Rutherford House, 2005.

———. "Concupiscence: Sin and the Mother of Sin," https:// heidelblog.net/2015/01/concupiscence-sin-and-the-mother-of-sin (accessed August 17, 2021).

———. "Heidelcast Series: Nomism and Antinomianism," https:// heidelblog.net/2018/08/heidelcast-series-nomism-and-antino mianism (accessed September 3, 2020).

———. "Revoice, Nashville, and the Therapeutic Revolution," https://heidelblog.net/2019/07/revoice-nashville-and-the-ther apeutic-revolution/ (accessed August 27, 2021).

Clowney, Edmund P. *Preaching Christ in All of Scripture.* Wheaton, IL: Crossway Books, 2003.

Diamant, Jeff. "Half of U.S. Christians Say Casual Sex between Consenting Adults Is Sometimes or Always Acceptable," https://www. pewresearch.org/fact-tank/2020/08/31/half-of-u-s-christians-say-casual-sex-between-consenting-adults-is-sometimes-or-always-acceptable/ (accessed August 31, 2020).

Dreher, Rod. "Falwell Family Values," https://www.theamerican conservative.com/dreher/falwell-family-values-kinky-pool-boy-affair-liberty-university (accessed August 25, 2020).

Erskine, Ralph. *The Works of Ralph Erskine.* Vol. 2. Glasgow: Free Presbyterian Publications, 1991.

ESV Study Bible. Wheaton, IL: Crossway Bibles, 2008.

Fee, Gordon D. *The First Epistle to the Corinthians*. The New International Commentary on the New Testament. Grand Rapids: Eerdmans, 1987.

Fee, Gordon D. *God's Empowering Presence: The Holy Spirit in the Letters of Paul*. Peabody, MA: Hendrickson Publishers, Inc., 1994.

Fitzmyer, Joseph A. *First Corinthians: A New Translation with Introduction and Commentary. The Anchor Yale Bible*. New Haven, CT: Yale University Press, 2008.

Gagnon, Robert. *The Bible and Homosexual Practice*. Nashville: Abingdon Press, 2001.

Galli, Mark. *Chaos and Grace: Discovering the Liberating Work of the Holy Spirit*. Grand Rapids: Baker Books, 2011.

Garland, David E. *1 Corinthians*. Baker Exegetical Commentary on the New Testament. Grand Rapids: Baker Academic, 2003.

Godet, Frederic Louis. *Commentary on First Corinthians*. Grand Rapids: Kregel Publications, 1985.

Goldsworthy, Graeme. *According to Plan: The Unfolding Revelation of God in the Bible*. Downers Grove, IL: InterVarsity Press, 1991.

———. *Gospel and Kingdom: A Christian Interpretation of the Old Testament*. Waynesboro, GA: Paternoster Press, 2000.

———. *Preaching the Whole Bible as Christian Scripture*. Grand Rapids: Eerdmans, 2000.

Hays, Richard B. *First Corinthians*. Interpretation: A Bible Commentary for Teaching and Preaching. Louisville: Westminster John Knox Press, 2011.

Heidelberg Catechism, The. Grand Rapids: Board of Publication of the Christian Reformed Church, 1976.

Heidelberg Catechism, 450th Anniversary Edition. The Synod of the Reformed Church in the United States, 2013.

Hodge, Charles. *Commentary on the First Epistle to the Corinthians*. Grand Rapids: William B. Eerdmans Publishing Company, 1980.

Horton, Michael. *Christless Christianity: The Alternative Gospel of the American Church*. Grand Rapids: Baker Books, 2008.

———. "Covenant," https://www.ligonier.org/learn/articles/cov enant (accessed August 27, 2020).

———. *For Calvinism*. Grand Rapids: Zondervan, 2011.

———. *Introducing Covenant Theology*. Grand Rapids: Baker, 2006.

———. "The God-centered Gospel," http://www.ligonier.org/learn/articles/god-centered-gospel.

———. *The Christian Faith*: A Systematic Theology for Pilgrims on the Way. Grand Rapids: Zondervan, 2011.

Hyde, Daniel R. *God in our Midst: The Tabernacle & Our Relationship with God*. Sanford, FL: Reformation Trust Publishing, 2012.

Jensen, Irving L. *Jensen's Survey of the New Testament*. Chicago: Moody, 1981.

Johnson, Dennis E. *Him We Proclaim: Preaching Christ from All the Scripture*. Phillipsburg, NJ: P&R Publishing, 2007.

Keller, Tim. "American Idols," http://www.christianitytoday.com/ct/2009/november/1.71.html.

Kistemaker, Simon J. *1 Corinthians*. New Testament Commentary Series. Grand Rapids: Baker, 1993.

Marshall, Walter. *The Gospel Mystery of Sanctification: Growing in Holiness by Living in Union with Christ*. Put into modern English by Bruce H. McRae. Eugene: Wipf and Stock, 2005.

Maschke, Timothy H. *Gathered Guests: A Guide to Worship in the Lutheran Church, Second Edition*. St. Louis: Concordia Publishing House, 2009.

M'Cheyne, Robert Murray. *A Basket of Fragments: Notes for Revival*. Scotland, UK: Christian Focus Publications, 1996.

Morris, Leon. *The Cross in the New Testament*. Grand Rapids: Eerdmans, 1965.

Murray, John. *Redemption Accomplished and Applied*. Grand Rapids: Eerdmans, 1955.

Newton, John. *The Works of John Newton*. Vol. 4. Carlisle, PA: The Banner of Truth Trust, 1988.

Noll, Stephen. *The Global Anglican Communion: Contending for Anglicanism 1993–2018*. Newport Beach, CA: Anglican House, 2018.

Null, Ashley. *Divine Allurement: Cranmer's Comfortable Words*. London: The Latimer Trust, 2014.

Owen, John. *The Works of John Owen*. William H. Goold, ed. Edinburgh: The Banner of Truth Trust, 1967.

Packer, J. I. *Keep in Step with the Spirit*. Grand Rapids: Revell, 1984.

———. *Knowing God*. Downers Grove, IL: InterVarsity Press, 1973.

Packer, J. I. and Gary A. Parrett. *Grounded in the Gospel: Building Believers the Old-Fashioned Way*. Grand Rapids: Baker, 2010.

Perkins, William. ed. Paul M. Smalley, Joel R. Beeke, and Derek W. H. Thomas. *The Works of William Perkins, Vol. 2.* Grand Rapids: Reformation Heritage Books, 2015.

Plass, Ewald. *What Luther Says: A Practical In-Home Anthology for the Active Christian.* St. Louis: Concordia Publishing House, 1959.

Powlison, David. *The Biblical Counseling Movement: History and Context.* Greensboro, NC: New Growth Press, 2010.

Prior, David. *The Message of 1 Corinthians.* The Bible Speaks Today. Downers Grove, IL: InterVarsity Press, 1985.

Psalter Hymnal: Doctrinal Standards and Liturgy. "Canons of Dort." Grand Rapids: Board of Publication of the Christian Reformed Church, 1976.

Purves, Andrew. *Reconstructing Pastoral Theology: A Christological Foundation.* Louisville: Westminster John Knox Press, 2004.

Rahlfs, Alfred, ed. *Septuaginta, Accordance Bible Software.* Stuttgart: Deutsche Bibelgesellschaft, 2006.

Roberts, Vaughan. *God's Big Picture: Tracing the Storyline of the Bible.* Downers Grove, IL: IVP Books, 2002.

Ryken, Philip Graham, Derek W. H. Thomas, and J. Ligon Duncan III, eds. *Give Praise to God: A Vision for Reforming Worship.* Phillipsburg, NJ: P&R Publishing, 2003.

Schaff, Philip, ed. *Nicene and Post-Nicene Fathers.* Vol. 3 of *A Select Library of the Christian Church.* Peabody, MA: Hendrickson Publishers, Inc., 2004.

Schenck, Kenneth. *1 & 2 Corinthians: A Commentary for Bible Students.* Indianapolis: Wesleyan Publishing House, 2006.

Smith, James K. A. *You Are What You Love: The Spiritual Power of Habit*. Grand Rapids: Brazos Press, 2016.

Stone, Jordan. *A Communion of Love: The Christ-Centered Spirituality of Robert Murray M'Cheyne*. Eugene, OR: Wipf & Stock, 2019.

Stott, John. *Same Sex Partnerships?: A Christian Perspective*. Grand Rapids: Revell, 1998.

The College of Bishops (ACNA). *Sexuality and Identity: A Pastoral Statement from the College of Bishops*, https://anglicanchurch.net/sexuality-and-identity-a-pastoral-statement-from-the-college-of-bishops/.

Thiselton, Anthony C. *The First Epistle to the Corinthians*, The New International Greek Testament Commentary. Grand Rapids: Eerdmans, 2000.

Ursinus, Zacharias. *The Commentary of Dr. Zacharias Ursinus on the Heidelberg Catechism*. Phillipsburg, NJ: Presbyterian and Reformed Publishing Company, NA.

Valk, Pieter. "Why Say Gay? A Response to 'Yes to Gay Identity, No to Gay Sex?,'" https://juicyecumenism.com/2021/04/20/gay-anglican-pieter-valk/ (accessed August 27, 2021).

Wanamaker, Charles A. *The Epistles to the Thessalonians: A Commentary on the Greek Text*. New International Greek Testament Commentary (Grand Rapids: Eerdmans, 1990).

Watson, Thomas. *A Body of Divinity*. Carlisle, PA: The Banner of Truth Trust, 1992.

Welch, Ed. *When People Are Big and God Is Small: Overcoming Peer Pressure, Codependency, and the Fear of Man*. Phillipsburg, NJ: Presbyterian and Reformed Publishing, 1997.

Westminster Larger Catechism. Glasgow: Free Presbyterian Publications, 2003.

Wilson, Geoffrey B. *Romans to Ephesians: New Testament Commentaries*. Vol. 1. Carlisle, PA: The Banner of Truth Trust, 2005.

Witherington III, Ben. *Conflict and Community in Corinth: A Socio-Rhetorical Commentary on 1 and 2 Corinthians*. Grand Rapids: Eerdmans, 1995.

Wright, Christopher J. H. *The Mission of God: Unlocking the Bible's Grand Narrative*. Downers Grove, IL: IVP Academic, 2006.